To place yourself in this position there are many travel advisors available; many you will find listed in "Destinations". In addition, it is a good idea to check with your local fly shop to see what saltwater fly fishing trips are offered.

BONEFISH
TARPON·PERMIT
Fly Fishing Guide

THE BIG THREE

Al Raychard

Frank
Amato
PORTLAND

Acknowledgments

No book covering an area as unique and diverse as the Caribbean, and fly fishing targets as special as bonefish, permit and tarpon could ever be undertaken without the help, assistance and expertise of numerous individuals. I wish it could be said that everything in these pages is based upon personal experience, knowledge and know-how, but the truth is, without the input from some kind and willing individuals, most of whom have far more experience than I, this book would have been much more difficult to complete. Thanks to them, the effort was much easier, and the final product better than I ever hoped for.

The same is true of certain fishing booking agents, tackle manufacturers and other folks in the industry. When I found myself in need of a product or travel arrangements for the purpose of fishing and taking photographs, or simply to renew old facts, they came through. Such willingness to help is much appreciated, and confirms my belief that the fly fishing industry is, indeed, a special family.

With that said, let me say this book is as much theirs as it is mine, and my deep thanks and gratitude go out to the following: Scott Heywood, Angling Adventures; Craig Johnston, M.D.; Doug Schlink, Angler Adventures; Mr. John Eustice. John Eustice Associates; Mr. Dick Born, Posada del Sol; Mr. Craig Hayes, Turneffe Flats; Mr. Jonathan Watts and Mr. Jack Simpson, Canada-Cuba Sports & Cultural Festivals; Captain Tony Traad, Homestead, Florida; Captain Dan Strub, Marathon, Florida; Mr. Tom McCullough, Cortland Line Company; Tracy Tallar, Ex-Officio Adventure Wear; Fisher Fly Rods; Dr. Jack Mermelstein, RMA Sunoptics, Inc.; Mr. Terry Ross, Tarponwear; Climax Leader Systems; Mr. Ken Menard, Umpqua Feather Merchants; Mr. Larry Valentine, Valentine Reel Company; Terry Gunn, photographer, Penn Fly Rods; Scientific Anglers; Mr. James Coury, Predator Sporting Equipment, Inc.; Mr. Brian O'Keefe, photographer; Jim Grandt, Grandt Custom Rods, Ltd.; and last, but certainly not least, Mr. Frank Amato, for his faith, and taking a chance with this Maine country boy.

Dedication

To Diane, a better and more patient fly fisher than I.
Thank you for being part of my dream.

Published in 1996 by Frank Amato Publications, Inc.
P.O. Box 82112, Portland, Oregon 97282
(503) 653-8108
All photos taken by the author unless otherwise noted.
Cover photos: Al Raychard
Cover "PERMIT" inset photo: Terry Gunn
Title page photo: Brian O'Keefe
Fly plate photo: Jim Schollmeyer
Flies provided by Umpqua Feather Merchants
Knot illustrations: Bill Herzog
Softbound ISBN: 1-57188-050-X   Softbound UPC: 0-66066-00246-4
Book Design: Tony Amato
Printed in Canada
1 3 5 7 9 10 8 6 4 2

CONTENTS

INTRODUCTION

The flats off Sandy Point, Abaco, Bahamas are some of the most extensive in the archipelago. Some stretch on for miles, and are rarely fished.
Facing Page: Flowers grace the landscape at Rio Colorado.

I am a New Englander born and bred, and I cut my fly fishing teeth on Maine's remote trout ponds and landlocked salmon, eventually graduating to more exotic species like Atlantic salmon, trophy brook trout in Labrador and Quebec and Arctic char. When I visited Alaska for the first time many years later, all seemed right with the world and I could not imagine or believe a more beautiful place, or better fly fishing for rainbow trout, among others, existed on earth. America's largest state is truly one of fly fishing's great combos, and no matter how many times I travel there it is never enough.

Pursuit of steelhead in the Deschutes and other fabled northwest rivers, introduced to me by good friend, noted photographer and angling writer Scott Ripley of Tigard, Oregon, was a true delight, too. The fish and working a fly for them remind me a great deal of fishing New Brunswick's Miramichi or some other Atlantic salmon run, and for that reason I felt right at home and have been an avid fan ever since. It saddens me to say because I live in the northeast and because of conflicting seasons on Atlantic salmon, brook trout, striped bass and other eastern species, I do not fish those fabled waters as much as I would like.

Each of these fish, and others I have encountered over the years, hold a special place in my heart, as do the places they reside, both urban and wild, whether close to home or a jet and float plane ride away. Each is special, unique and a challenge as well as a joy to hunt with a fly rod, and I count my blessings. Time and means have afforded me the opportunity to get to know and appreciate them. It has been a fun and memorable ride, and I would not have missed it for the world.

But things change. Interests change. Whether in life or fly fishing, and for many of us life is fly fishing; whether we like it or not our journey is one of progressions, a journey of steps that take us from one level to the next. As a fly fisherman, the difficult thing I have found is to hold on to the past, to remember from where I came and to find time to fish those places and species which started it all as new passions come my way.

That is the situation I find myself in today. I still experience divine elation in fishing small, intimate brook trout ponds in Maine, and I pray to God Almighty I never go an entire season without visiting a favorite Atlantic salmon haunt. And while I have caught my share of dinosaur brook trout in the wilderness bastions of the far north, I find with growing frequency these days my mind and heart drift towards warmer climates. In a nut-

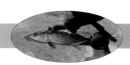

shell, since I hooked and landed my first bonefish in the Florida Keys, was manhandled by my first tarpon at the mouth of the Rio Colorado in Costa Rica and marveled over how much line and backing a permit can rip off a reel in skinny water, this country boy from Maine has never been the same!

To say that lately I have neglected the fish and places which initiated me to the world of fly fishing for the pursuit of bonefish, tarpon and permit is somewhat true. I hold them no less dear, but over the past years old freshwater haunts have grown less familiar, and I have become an addict when it comes to fishing the flats and exploring tepid waters. In my mind, even now in early March as an ice-storm hardens the landscape outside my window and I have recently returned from Posada del Sol on the island of Guanaja, just off the north coast of Honduras, my heart longs to be back there, or some place like it. Not just to escape the cold and ice which grips my northern home, for June and September are favorite times as well, but to again cast a fly in the lucid waters of the Caribbean, to hunt its flats and to partake of that special world and the myriad of experiences it affords. There is nothing which quite compares with the place, or the three popular game fish which inhabit its waters. My only salvation is knowing I will return in just a few weeks to take up the hunt once more.

To say my interest in these fish has been a learning experience would be an understatement, and one of the things I cherish most about these three is they are always teaching, pushing their challenger to do better, be better, yet each can be such a joyous surprise. Each is blessed with some of the keenest eyesight and most acute hearing of any fish on the flats, and each can be as skittish and reluctant to accept a fly as any fish I have ever met, even when the angler assumes everything has been done right. Yet at times, these demons, these phantoms of the flats can be almost congenial, as if willing to play the game. While always cautious and capable of disappearing as fast as they appear I have experienced divine instances when success was far less than difficult, almost easy, particularly with bones and tarpon. Such times are infrequent when fishing for permit, the most intense and difficult of the "Big Three" to take on a fly in my opinion, but even these ghost-like denizens have their moments when they break all their own rules and give the angler a break.

But as I sit here on this winter's day, reliving visits and experiences past while pondering with great anticipation those yet to come, it matters not in which mode I find them, or where. The important thing is they grace a magical part of our world I find mesmerizing and therapeutic to both body and soul, a part of our world that would be so empty without them. They are available and willing participants, even when under the most frustrating of conditions and circumstances, and they are waiting to offer some of the most challenging and demanding yet rewarding even surprising fly fishing on the planet. That is all that matters, all that counts.

If you have not yet done so I invite you to take up the challenge, to become part of that world, but do so with a warning that a price will be paid. Not in monetary terms, or in the hours of frustration generally invested before success comes your way, for the dividends are great and are returned in kind ten-fold the first time you hook up, and they only get better. But in the sense you will never be the same, nor will other fly fishing pursuits you have known or consider dear, and you will never get enough. Like a drug it gets under your skin, and once hooked it is a lifelong compliance.

So take it from someone who knows. These fish, and their environs, not only change perspectives and priorities, but they never let you go. That is the price you must be willing to pay.

But if you don't believe me, then consider this. According to one source an angler by the name of J.P. McFerran of Louisville, Kentucky, whether by accident or design, is said to have landed the first bonefish on rod and reel in the Florida Keys back in 1891. In a letter to W.H. Gregg, author of an article on the account which appeared in "Where, When and How to Catch Fish On The East Coast Of Florida" in 1902, McFerron states, "I verily believe that, pound for pound, the Bonefish is, far and away, the King of all swimmers and the only objection I can urge against him is that an experience with him disqualifies one for all other fishing."

And if that is not enough, it was Zane Grey who, during one of those rare times was at a loss for words, wrote in "*The Bonefish Brigade*," I have never been able to tell why it (angling for bone fish) seems the fullest, the most difficult, the strangest and most thrilling, the lonesomest and most satisfying of all kinds of angling."

Nothing more need be said.

Al Raychard
(March, 1995) Saco, Maine

BONEFISH

It is not well known among modern aficionados, but the game of chasing bonefish with rod and reel in the Caribbean basin is almost as old as the story of American dry fly fishing itself. As early as 1906, about the same time Theodore Gordon helped usher in the Golden Years of the Catskills, a young guide by the name of Preston Pinder poled his wooden skiff across the flats of Upper Matecumbe Key in south Florida. In the bow sat Senator William Thompson Martin of Kentucky, eighty-three years young at the time, and, although bonefish had been caught on rod and reel years earlier, reputedly he was the first guided bone fisherman known to angling history.

Although the senator was armed with a bait-casting rod, used a piece of crab for bait and was defeated in his initial quest the idea of stalking the flats for bonefish had begun, and since then scores have followed. Indeed, few other fish have been elevated to notoriety so quickly, and perhaps more than any other game fish with the exception of Atlantic salmon, steelhead and billfish, few are besieged by such a dedicated following that would sell body and soul to spend more time in their pursuit.

It can be said the ache and desire to stalk this fish more and more once contact has been made is downright scary. The bonefish and the world in which it lives clearly has the ability to change lives and perspectives, and I know enthusiasts—nut cases really—who have quit jobs with bright futures, divorced wives and left home just to dedicate more time to this fish and its shallow-water home. While most don't go to such extremes, it is difficult not to dream or ponder the idea, this fish has attracted devoted enthusiasts

Scott Heywood of Sheridan, Wyoming with a bonefish taken near Crooked Island, Bahamas.

from all walks of life. The bonefish is not discriminatory or discerning in its treatment of Homo sapiens, and, depending upon its mood and circumstances, treats all who seek them with the same lack of respect and tenacity, at other times with a degree of gentleness and congeniality—among other characteristics on a long list—regardless of social status. This is just one of their more redeeming qualities and a personality trait which makes bonefish one of the top angling thrills in shallow water, as well as a target for all who take up the challenge.

The rise to fame and popularity of the bonefish as an ultimate fly fishing quest is a relatively new phenomenon. Although their presence on Caribbean flats has been known among anglers since long before the turn of the century, and their pursuit with rod and reel a known opportunity for nearly as long, except for a handful of fortunate souls who lived or vacationed in the area, the many attributes of this fish were not well known until the 1950s. Even then, and well into the 1960s poling, wading and working the flats was pretty much considered somewhat of an oddity. It was known, and it was done, but the dedicated fraternity was small, and it would be another decade or so until the pursuit of this fish began to reach universal attention.

But it can still be said, even now despite all the angling hoopla and acclaim over this marvelous resource, surprisingly little is actually known about this "ghost" of the flats. Much of the industry attention in recent years has been dedicated to the perfection of tackle and techniques, of informing the growing hordes where and when to go. In our haste to cater to those growing numbers we have pretty much forgotten about the fish

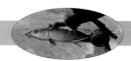

The author plays a bonefish in the Marls, Abaco, Bahamas. It has proven to be one of the author's favorite spots in the Bahamas.

Bonefish like this six-pounder taken on Guanaja Island are swimming muscles of power and stamina.
This is a large fish for the Bay Islands, and though not easy to take are worth the effort and wait.

itself. Other than being equipped with tackle better suited to the task, having more know-how between our ears of how to entice them to the fly, and raving over its guile and tenacity, most who stalk the flats these days know as little about the bonefish as our predecessors did at the turn of the century.

The bonefish is a member of the family *Albulidae* (Order *Elopiformes*). This is one of the most ancient of *teleostean* fishes, fish with a bony rather than cartilaginous skeleton; fossils of an extinct species, *Albula antigua* dating back more than 120 million years to the Cretaceous period have been discovered in Florida, and fossils of other *albulids* have been found in many parts of the world dating back 125 million years. It is difficult to say with certainty whether evolution has greatly changed the outward appearance of this fish over time, but it is doubtful, and it is safe to say the examples we hunt today and take on flies throughout the Caribbean look much as their ancestors did.

It is now known bonefish have a global distribution and that several species exist, all in tropical or semi-tropical waters, roughly between 30 degrees North and 30 degrees South of the Equator. Those found in the Caribbean basin are *Albula vulpes*. Translated the name appropriately means "white fox," undoubtedly due to it sometimes whitish appearance in the water and sly, cunning demeanor, outward nervousness and speed. Another species, *Albula nemoptera,* or longfin bonefish, is found

on the Atlantic and Pacific coasts of the Americas, as well as the Caribbean. It is rarely caught by sport fishermen in Florida or the Bahamas, or anywhere else for that matter, but is rather common in Jamaica and other locales south to Venezuela. *A. nemoptera* is small in size, the largest examples running 13 to 14 inches in length, and its dorsal fin sprouts a long, whip-like dorsal ray, much like that on tarpon.

Other species include *Albula neoguinaica* and *Albula glossodorta,* found in Hawaiian and Indo-West Pacific waters. Several so-called deep water varieties have also been documented, *Pterothrissus belloci* and *P. gissu.* They are most common in West and South Africa and off the coast of Japan, and carry an elongated dorsal fin that extends along 60 percent of the total body length.

In outward appearance, bonefish are truly a vision of divine splendor and near perfect aerodynamic design with a bluish-green hue along the back, and sides covered with a bright silver to whitish mail of scales descending to a near milky-white belly. Mother Nature, in her infinite wisdom, has done a marvelous job in providing more than adequate camouflage to these shallow-swimmers, for the dark and spotted back mixes well with the mottled sea floor as human eyes look down upon them, while at the same time the white belly reflects sunlight off the bottom. There are times, too many in fact, when these fish

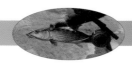

appear out of nowhere and then disappear into oblivion so quickly the angler has no time to respond, much less than make a cast.

The ability of bonefish to appear and vanish is nothing short of amazing, and it is to the hunter's advantage this is not a motionless fish, taking up stations like trout and salmon in deep moving currents, for it would be even more difficult to spot them under sun-blasted water on a carpet of turtle grass or mixed coral and sand. It is also a blessing they are not always alert and prone to mistakes. Were it otherwise, these fish would be even more difficult to hook. As it is, detecting motion, a moving silhouette or ghost-like shadow over clear sand, or a tail and dorsal fin protruding from the surface as they feed, is often the only telltale sign bones are in the area or within casting reach. And it is this combination of silver and bluish-green—much like the environs in which it lives—which allows the bonefish to appear invisible at times, and difficult to spot among novice enthusiasts, even with the aid of polarized sunglasses.

Many bonefish have pearly reflections around the head, while parts of the fins, as well as the pig-like snout may show a yellowish or dusky color. The large, sail-like dorsal fin, generally the same bluish-green color as the back but more transparent, consists of 17-20 soft rays. The anal fin has 8-9 soft rays, the ventral fin 9 and the pectoral fin 15-17. The sides of the bonefish are noticeably covered with scales, and there may be as many as 65-73 along the lateral line, depending upon age and size. There are no scales on the head.

Several other body characteristics quickly become apparent when the angler has time to study the bonefish up close, generally after a successful battle as the fish rests in appreciating hands before being released. One is its shape. Bonefish are elongated, somewhat like a torpedo, and because of that fact they are able to travel and feed in extremely shallow water. Most activity is in depths of one to two feet, depending upon the tide, but it is not uncommon to spot whole schools on a feeding spree—perhaps 100 to 200 fish—even larger solitary loners in much skinnier locales.

While fishing Bernard Cay in the Bahamas with Scott Heywood, a travel consultant in the angling arena out of Sheridan, Wyoming and bonefish enthusiast if there ever was one, I happened to be working a seldom visited flat when I suddenly came upon a solitary bonefish which seemed to be just sitting on top of the water. The action and opportunity had been good that morning, and it wasn't exactly a revelation to see another fish, but what took me by surprise is where I saw it. The water was less than ankle deep, and the lone monster was so big half its sides and all of its back protruded from the water. At first I thought the fish had been marooned by the ebbing tide, for it kept teetering from side to side like a small boat on rough seas, but then it would push forward a foot or two with great swipes of the tail, before stopping again. I was totally spellbound by the sight, but after several steps and closer observation I realized the fish was actively feeding, sucking up tidbits like a vacuum cleaner off the bottom. Just as I realized what was

going on and prepared to lift my rod the fish turned and like a bullet took off across the flat creating a massive wake and spraying water as it went! I never did get off a cast, but that event imprinted into my brain the fact that anglers hunting the flats should never be surprised where they might find these fish, regardless of size, and it is a truism they might be found just about anywhere, even in the thinnest of water!

Another obvious characteristic the bonefish enthusiast cannot help but notice is the tail. It is large, almost too large when compared to body size. Like most speedsters the bonefish sports a deeply forked rear propulsion system designed for fast accelerations rather than power. With just a series of rapid flicks they can boost from a slow cruising mode, or from a standby position while feeding to sizzling bursts of speed that enable them to cover the length of a football field in seconds. The top tail fin is generally as long as the dorsal fin is high, and when "mudding," or "tailing" in shallow water, the terms used to describe when bonefish tip downward to feed along the bottom, the tail thrusts upwards and protrudes above the surface. Along with its excited back and forth movement and splashing, a bright reflection of sun off the tail is a dead give-away bonefish are present and actively feeding.

In many situations, however, despite their size, the tail of a bonefish, even those from an entire pod of several hundred fish, is not always easy to see. A shallow flat is a mirror of glare and reflection, and the tails of mudding fish are extremely well camouflaged. When hunting a flat it often helps to bend low and scan two to four inches above the water, particularly when the surface is rippled. It also helps to keep in mind, the larger the fish, the longer the tail and the higher it protrudes above the water. If fishing water knee deep or so, and the tail or tails extend above the surface, chances are it is a large fish Also, the size of tailing bonefish has a direct correlation to water depth. Larger bonefish cannot dip down to forage in extremely skinny locales, so I look for the bigger examples in areas with at least 12 to 15 inches of water. This does not mean to say large bonefish will not explore and utilize shallower flats. They will and often do. But it has been an observation on many occasions in water less than a foot deep, the skinnier the water the smaller the fish are apt to be.

And finally, don't forget permit also frequent the flats, and it is not uncommon for novice bonefish enthusiasts to confuse the tails of these fish with bonefish. I have done so myself on more than one occasion. It helps to remember permit are rather deep bellied, so they cannot take advantage of extremely shallow feeding areas and will seldom travel where their backs are exposed above the surface. Permit, especially the larger examples, are generally found in places where the water is about two-feet deep or better. Nonetheless, these two denizens are often found on the same flats, and a good way to differentiate one from the other is to remember the tail of a bonefish appears silver, or transparent. The tail of a permit, however, appears black and, unlike that of a bonefish, the dorsal fin is more sickle-shaped, and also appears dark or black.

Dr. Ron Apter of Falls Church, Virginia looks for bonefish in the Marls. This area is one of the most bonefish-rich areas in the Bahamas and is where the author caught his largest bonefish, weighing in at eleven pounds and measuring 31 inches from head to tail.

The mouth of this fish is also interesting. It is not exceptionally large and is situated on the bottom, beneath a long, conical shaped snout-like nose, and is rimmed by soft but leathery-tough tissue. The inside of the mouth is just as tough, with the tongue and palate covered with hundreds of small, hard beads or bubbles. These are actually "pharyngeal teeth" which assist in the process of breaking down food before ingestion. At the back and on both sides of the tongue are a set of powerful crushers which enables the bonefish to demolish clams and other hard-shelled foods with relative ease.

All this is somewhat unimportant to the angler, except for two points. One is size. Although bonefish can accurately be described as opportunistic feeders, scavengers in fact, and will dine on a host of foods they seem to prefer small to medium-sized tidbits. The most productive flies, therefore, are also more often than not in the small to medium range—less than two-and-one-half inches overall—and similar in size to the most desired natural foods.

The other point is toughness. Because the mouth and lip area of these critters is like shoe leather it is important all hooks be honed to a fine point. Deep penetration is essential, and hook points filed in the shape of a triangle or diamond providing three or four cutting edges work well. Even barbless hooks, which are becoming more common on the flats these days, penetrate deep when honed this way, not only on bones, but tarpon, permit and other flats species as well. There is an ongoing debate among some enthusiasts, however, that hooks shaped this way have too many sharp edges and have a tendency to cut all the way through during a long fight. In the

years that I filed hooks this way I never found that to be true, but now I generally hone just one side of the point as if forming the first edge on a triangular point. It seems to penetrate just as well and is easier and takes less time to do.

Of all the obvious physical features of the bonefish perhaps the most interesting, and one of the least understood, are its eyes, particularly its adipose eyelids. To say the least these fish have keen eyesight, and when presented right can see a fly as it descends to the bottom, or sits on the floor of a sand flat from several yards away. They can also distinguish color, up to 24 hues in a narrow band, making the color of flies important from location to location, flat to flat, even hour to hour based upon available foods, light conditions and other factors.

Even more interesting is the fact that, unlike most fish, the eyeball of the bonefish is not exposed, but covered with a smooth, tough, transparent sheath or membrane. This covering has a tiny opening centered above the pupil and allows the bonefish to literally bury its head in the mud and sand to seek out food without obstructing its vision. Without question this asset is a major factor in the behavior of this fish, and key to what allows it to be such a proficient bottom feeder. It has also been suggested this sheath helps polarize sunlight enabling the bonefish to hunt, plunder and feed under clear, bright skies, which they often do. It might reduce turbulence around the eyes providing the bonefish with clear vision when swimming at high speeds.

DISTRIBUTION

Bonefish are global in range, inhabiting nearly all tropical and semi-tropical waters roughly within 30-degrees North and South of the Equator. They are found in the Pacific, most notably around Christmas Island, and are known from the Cook Islands to Hawaii to the west coast of Mexico and Central America, where they extend from Culiacan north of Mazatlan south all the way to Panama. At the present time, except for Christmas Island and some exploring now going on in Panama and a couple other spots, there is little developed fishing for bonefish in the Pacific and much remains to be discovered.

Here in the western Atlantic, however, the opposite is quite true. Hunting of this fish with angling gear has been going on since about the turn of the century and there are literally dozens of places the modern enthusiast can visit to take up the challenge. As a whole, the Caribbean represents the world's greatest concentration of bonefish. They are found from one end of the basin to the other. Starting on the Yucatan Peninsula of Mexico, these silver demons are found in Belize south to Honduras. An increasing number of reports keep coming in of populations along the coast of Nicaragua, and, along with parts of the Honduran coast, it could very well be this area is one of the last great bonefish frontiers yet to be explored. There seems to be few along the coast of Costa Rica. There is little doubt a certain few are present, although personally I

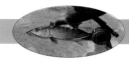

have yet to discover any while on several tarpon excursions there. They are present in Panama, but that country has yet to be considered a viable destination, undoubtedly due to the lack of established fishing camps, although Venezuela has long been considered one of the region's great hotspots.

To the north bonefish are found from about Biscayne Bay in south Florida to Key West. Bonefish are also found throughout the vast Bahama archipelago and in fact, no place else in the western Atlantic, or perhaps on Earth, will the bonefish hunter find more accessible flats or greater concentrations of bonefish. Cuba also has a fair number, and for years, until travel was restricted, places like Isla de Pinos south of Havana and a couple other spots produced some of the best angling in the Caribbean. Heavy netting has taken its toll in some of these places, but there are still good numbers, and some large examples at that, particularly off Cuba's south coast in the "Garden of the Queens" about 50 miles off shore from the small port of Jucaro. I have been fortunate enough to fish there twice, for both bonefish and tarpon, and I dare say when this country finally becomes accessible to Americans again, which I hope is soon, that string of mangrove and coral islets will become a hot destination.

South of Cuba, bonefish are common in the Caymans, particularly Little Cayman; Jamaica, Haiti, Puerto Rico and throughout the long string of Lesser Antilles, including St. Thomas, the British Virgin Islands, Antigua, Guadeloupe, Martinique, St. Vincent and Barbados.

While bonefish are well represented throughout the Caribbean, it should not be taken for granted that this species

Home-away-from-home, while fishing Cuba's Garden of the Queen's, is a 65-foot mother ship right out of Hemingway's day. From there fisermen travel to the flats in skiffs.

is found everywhere. While certain places seem to teem with them, in others not a one can be found. This is true even on the same island, one side may offer great angling opportunities while on the other wetting a line is nothing more than a waste of time. Bonefish, like all fish, have certain requirements. Ample food supplies, proper water temperatures and specific habitat needs. The myriad of islands and small keys within the Caribbean, and the miles of indented and irregular coastline along the mainland countries are divinely blessed with all the commodities this species needs to survive, but its greatest asset is the thousands of square miles of shallow flats.

Above all else this is a shallow water inhabitant, and it is this one attribute which sets the Caribbean apart as a bonefish mecca. Other places in the world have flats and bonefish, but comparatively, or even collectively they are small to what is available within the Caribbean basin. Within the 500-mile long Bahama archipelago there are some 70,000 square miles of shoal and flat water alone, the vast majority of which contains bonefish, and it is still possible to discover and explore unknown waters. There are some 4,000 square miles of flats along the Florida Keys. The amount along the Yucatan and Belize could easily be double that, and that is just a small part of what this rich and unique area has to offer.

New and productive areas of the Caribbean are being discovered with regularity and there appears to be no end in sight as to where bonefish are found. A bonefish addict could spend a lifetime here exploring, discovering and fishing and not visit a place more than once, yet leave behind new waters still to be seen. What a life that would be! But shallow water is the key. Without its extensive flats and shoals, the Caribbean might offer great fishing, but not for bones, and I pray this angler is long gone before Mother Earth, in her ever-changing ways, alters the character of this place to the point it is no longer the heaven for bonefish that presently it is. I believe there is little for me to worry about.

LIFE CYCLE

It is interesting to note as we embark on a new century, particularly in light of the global awareness and popularity of bonefish as a fly fishing target and the volumes of written material now available, how little is actually known of its life cycle. While new places to explore, innovative angling techniques and strategies and equipment better designed for the task seem to come with each new season, the scientific and angling world remains in the shadows to a great degree as to the reproduction of the bonefish and its early life history.

What is known is rather basic. According to one source, studies in various parts of its Caribbean range suggest spawning is apt to occur throughout the calendar year. The theory is supported by the fact that ripe or near ripe adults are found in the Florida Keys in spring and summer as well as fall and winter. On the other hand, studies in the Bahamas have shown spawning occurs there in the fall, primarily in November and

December, although some Bahamian guides claim spawning takes place from April through early June. No one seems to know for sure. Considering most bonefish populations are local in nature, traveling from shallow water to deep water within their local range depending upon water temperatures and weather conditions, there is a good chance spawning takes place at different times of the year within the Caribbean basin. Again, this is only speculation on my part based on personal discovery of ripe adults in Biscayne Bay in April and May but at different times of year in other locales.

In the larva stage of life it is known as *leptocephalus,* and at this point, it is elongated, thin and except for the head nearly transparent, these someday-to-be bonefish look nothing like their adult counterparts. It is believed these youngsters spend much of their early life in shallow water, but at some point tread into deeper areas and may be dispersed by ocean currents. Following an initial growth stage, these young fish experience a unique shrinking stage during which they transform into a bonefish-like appearance, followed by a second growth stage, after which they reach adulthood.

Clearly more study has to be done. No resource is infinite, even in an area the size of the Caribbean basin. In some areas bonefish have been netted and commercially fished to severe lows, and while recreational angling pressure is minimal, considering the strict practice of catch and release at nearly all lodges and the same philosophy shared by the majority of anglers in general, the loss and degradation of habitat and water quality in some spots remains a real threat. To ensure this special fish is with us in years to come, we need to know more about its early life cycle in case protective measures need to be taken.

SIZE

It is the cherished desire of every angler who stalks the flats, to hook into a truly large bonefish. Better yet, to hook into several. This is truly a fish where bigger is better, for it is the bigger examples which not only generate more rod-bending power and speed once on the fly, but which take more time to win the day.

Part of the problem is finding large bonefish, something in the eight to 10 pound range or larger, in sufficient numbers so the angler has an even chance at success. On the average these fish run two to seven pounds in most Caribbean locales, and while larger examples certainly exist they are not as common as their smaller counterparts. It seems the size of bonefish is relative to the area being fished, while in other areas timing is the key. To increase the chances of success for the largest examples it is to the angler's advantage to know where to go, and when to go.

If it is large bonefish that are of primary interest several destinations quickly come to mind. South Florida and the Florida Keys are home to some of the Caribbean's biggest bones, but keep in mind that the further south one travels along this emerald chain bonefish numbers generally diminish. With that in

The author and a small Florida bone. Even fish of this size can be a challenge and are a joy to catch on light tackle. Bonefish of this size are common throughout the Caribbean.

mind, Biscayne Bay, particularly in April and May, within the shadows of greater Miami and its hustle and bustle has historically produced some of the world's largest bonefish, and would be high on my list of big-bone hotspots. The action is seldom fast, nor are the fish easy to get on the fly, but with the assistance of an experienced area guide few places offer a better chance at hooking a trophy bone! Other areas in the Keys to give serious consideration to include the waters of Key Largo and Upper Matecumbe and Lower Matecumbe Key around Islamorada.

But the Keys are not the only place where it is possible to find and challenge large bonefish. In fact, if I had to pick just one area to seek out trophy bones it would undoubtedly be the Bahamas. This is big bonefish heaven, and places like Andros Island, Sandy Point and Marsh Harbor, Crooked Island, and Bimini in March and April are all places recognized for producing some of the Caribbean's largest bonefish. As they are in Biscayne Bay the bonefish in many of these spots are well educated, are not always cooperative and are rarely easy to fool with a fly, but few places offer as many big fish on such a consistent basis.

Other places are home to a good number of large bonefish as well. The flats near the outside reefs of Turneffe Island in Belize, Los Roques off the coast of Venezuela and one of my favorite places, the "Garden of the Queens" off the south coast of Cuba produce fish in the seven, eight and ten-pound range with fair consistency. And it is a fair statement to say I have been able to find at least a few large fish just about everywhere I have traveled. While some locales seem to have more than their share, it seems most places have a few, providing the angler at least an opportunity to take up the challenge. All the angler has to do is find them.

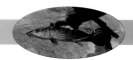

Smaller bonefish seem to travel in schools numbering a handful to several hundred, the big boys tend to be more solitary. As if bestowing a non-social behavior they cling to themselves, even if a school of smaller fish is on the same flat actively feeding. Because of this fact, the bigger bonefish are almost always more cautious and wary, and therefore more difficult to approach and require more tact. They are also more sensitive to the way a fly is delivered, and because of less competition for available food supplies, are typically more selective and less readily willing to accept your offering. For these reasons, plus the fact larger bonefish simply provide a more rewarding spectacle once hooked, hunting and successfully hooking a trophy bonefish is one of the ultimate challenges on the flats.

A couple things should be kept in mind when hunting the larger, solitary bonefish. The first is don't be surprised where you might find them. Despite their larger size big bones will often be found in the skinniest of water, and unless visibly tailing, they might not provide any telltale sign of their presence making it possible to walk right up on them. Doing so invariably will cause them to spook. Scout a flat before moving out, ideally starting in close and scanning no more than 30 to 40 yards ahead since even the trained eye might have difficulty detecting a single fish further away than that. And when working a flat, always work slow, letting your eyes be your guide. Regardless of fish size, or numbers of fish visibly seen or not seen, you are hunting.

In general, however, the biggest bones like slightly deeper water than their smaller counterparts, something from ankle to just below knee deep. Such depths provide several assets large fish like, including more freedom in their search for food, added assurance of more overhead cover, plus it allows them to tip downward to root and feed along the bottom. This is called "tailing," or "mudding," and it soon becomes apparent the size of the bonefish is directly related or in proportion to water depth. If the water is too shallow, say just a few inches, the big boys cannot tip down to feed so deeper water is to be given first priority. Also, when working ankle to knee-deep flats and a tailing fish is spotted, scan a couple inches above the surface and look for the tail. If the tail extends just above the surface, or barely breaks the surface, chances are it is a small fish, still worthy of a cast and some time perhaps, but small. On the other hand, if the tail appears high and extends well above the surface, and sits like a sail on the water, it is what you have been looking for. In a nutshell, the larger the tail and the more it extends above the surface in deep water the bigger the fish.

There are times, however, when one or more large specimens will be mixed in with small pods of fish. In this situation the angler has a choice based upon the scenery. He can seek out the largest in the school or one of the smaller members. If you go for the latter, the task can be somewhat easier, since it is the small bones that have a tendency to be less wary, more competitive for food and therefore more susceptible to a well placed fly, and they are often more spread out providing an opportunity to make a cast and achieve ultimate success. The largest members in the group will most likely be in the lead and may also pro-

vide for a cast or two, if so take advantage of the situation, but there is a good chance a number of small fish or sentries surround them making it difficult to get off a strategic cast. Whatever the case, the angler must quickly size up the situation and make his choice. Whether the largest bonefish happens to be alone or at the lead of a large school, hooking one is rarely easy, but doing so, or having the opportunity of trying is what bonefishing is all about.

While it is the larger bonefish which really get my adrenaline pumping and which take an increasing amount of my time, much can be said for those in the two to five or six pound class as well. Bonefish in this weight range make up the largest percentage of fish the angler will encounter throughout the Caribbean, and despite their smaller size, they still pack one heck of a punch on light tackle. Pound for pound no fish on the flats can slice water with such speed and determination and the smaller fish are no different in that respect than larger counterparts. The runs may not be as long, or the power as great, and the battle may not last as long. But in their own right small bonefish are no less exciting on the end of the line, and for every eight or nine-pound bonefish caught, it is generally possible to take several in the two to five-pound range.

This does not mean to say fish of this size are always easy to catch. In fact, they rarely are. Because they travel in schools and the fierce competition for food, small bones are generally more receptive to a well placed fly, but careful approach, tact and proper presentation are still paramount rules of the game.

Flowers grace the surroundings of Posada del Sol.

Throughout the Caribbean, most flats contain bonefish of various size, some small, some large with a certain size class predominating. For example, in Belize and the Yucatan although examples up to eight and 10-pounds are quite possible most are from one to perhaps four pounds. Around the island of Guanaja off the coast of Honduras, one to four pound fish are also the norm, although I have hooked into fish of about eight pounds. In the Florida Keys the bonefish tend to run big, but there are fewer of them than in many other locales in the Caribbean basin. In the Bahamas and Cuba, bonefish of all sizes are a good possibility, although in many specific locales they tend to run bigger than average. At Los Roques in Venezuela, there are numerous fish in the two to five-pound class, but this is also a good destination for bones from seven to 10-pounds.

WATER TEMPERATURES AND SEASONS

There is nothing quite as therapeutic as wading the flats. I live in the north, and even in March and April, times when pursuit of bonefish in the Caribbean is starting to peak, our waters are frigid and still clogged with ice. To escape to warmer climates and slide through tepid water is to experience heaven on earth, and little else rejuvenates the winter soul and helps the body come alive quite the same way.

From that perspective it is easy to understand why the bonefish resides in the Caribbean in the numbers it does. Throughout the region water temperatures rarely drop to below 60^0F and for much of the year temperatures are even warmer. For a fish that prefers warm surroundings, there is no better place to prod for food and call home.

Like all fish, however, *Abula vulpes* is sensitive to high and low temperature extremes. While a few are apt to be found on the flats when the temperature is between 69 and 72-degrees they are often hesitant to cooperate, and when the water is cooler they seem to be nonexistent. Between 73-degrees and 85-degrees bonefish seem to be everywhere and are most actively feeding, so this is considered "prime time" to be on the flats. At the higher end, they will tolerate temperatures from 86 to 89-degrees, but there seems to be fewer fish in this range, and above 90-degrees many desert the flats altogether, generally heading for deeper water.

When planning a fishing trip the angler should keep in mind several factors influence water temperature, including things as simple as time of year to more complex factors as cold fronts and wind. From about early July through much of September the wind is hardly a whisper throughout much of the Caribbean, and cold fronts, which can force water temperatures to tumble in the Florida Keys by a dozen degrees in February and early March, are nonexistent. The sun is also high and intense at this time, the sky clear except for brief periods of rain or showers, and water temperatures on the flats are well past 90-degrees, particularly at low tide. For these reasons, the summer months are among the poorest for the angler looking for consistent action in many locales.

By the same token, late December through February are not the greatest times either in semi-tropical areas like the Florida Keys and the Bahamas. It is possible to find bonefish, not only in good numbers but of large size in some places, but unstable cold fronts and cooling winds fluctuate shallow water temperatures, and fish move in and out depending upon the conditions. Fish may be present on a flat one day, or even part of a day, and not the next. In a nutshell, the fishing may be good or poor, all at the discretion of Mother Nature.

On the other end of the scale, there are generally two periods which are more predictable and reliable throughout much of the Caribbean. By the middle of March cold fronts and strong winds are starting to become less of a factor, and shallow water temperatures are starting to rise to a more comfortable range and become more stable. Due to these changes bonefish start to show with more regularity and continue to be present for longer periods of time. April is even better, May can be excellent and early June is quite good as well.

The other period is in the fall, September, October and November, and into early December if the weather holds. During this time wind is less of a factor, the water is generally clear and the heat of summer has started to wane. Water temperatures cool and drop into the more preferred range and bones are again more numerous on the flats in growing numbers. They will remain so all through the months of September and October, which typically offer the best fall angling, until water temperatures get too cold, or cold fronts and other weather conditions make things unpredictable. This generally happens during November and December, but even then a few days of warm weather will invite bones back to the flats, although they may not be as plentiful and when the weather turns again they will quickly disappear.

There are, of course, exceptions to all this, and there are times even during the heat of summer when bonefish may be found on the flats. There are also locations where fish seem to be present in good numbers and the angling opportunities quite reliable year-round.

For example, a rising tide can cool water temperatures on a flat sufficiently enough to allow bonefish a brief feeding spree even in July, August and September. In most areas and situations the best fishing during this period is during the early morning or late afternoon and evening hours, before and after the sun is at its strongest point. Keep an eye on the tides at this time. If they are rising or high during these hours, giving the flats a try is well advised. The angler should keep in mind, too, water temperatures can also vary from one area to another on the same flat regardless of season. Clear, sandy areas reflect the sun and are cooler than darker areas full of grass. When water temperatures are on the high side, particularly during the summer or when the sun is strong but the water is shallow, the cooler sandy flats should be given first priority. While in the winter, during cold spells or when water temperatures are generally on the cool side the darker areas should be considered first.

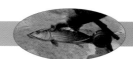

And keep in mind bonefish are permanent residents at many locations through the Caribbean basin: Andros Island, Abaco Island and other spots throughout the Bahamas, around the island of Guanaja in Honduras, at Turneffe Flats and Ambergris Cay in Belize and Los Roques off Venezuela, to name but a few. Bonefish are present in these areas through the calendar year, but these are considered semi-tropical locales, which means water temperatures do fluctuate from one part of the year to the next.

In general, however, the further south you travel, the more water temperatures remain pretty-much consistent, or stay within the preferred temperature range of bonefish longer, or cool for shorter periods of time, if at all. From January through early March water temperatures, and therefore the angling opportunities, are apt to be better in Venezuela or the southern end of the Bahamas than in the Florida Keys or northern end of the Bahamas where cold fronts, wind and other factors have a greater influence on water temperatures.

In some ways bonefishing, like all fishing is a crapshoot. You plan your trip, make your arrangements, you go and take what you get. Some who know the Caribbean far better than I might disagree, and while it is possible to find action in a great many locales year-round, and even though the chances of finding and taking big fish in some locales might be better at certain times than others, I always strive to plan my trips between March and late June, and from mid-September through November. It is during these periods when water temperatures and weather conditions seem to cooperate, when the greatest numbers of bonefish are on the flats and everything seems to come together. I have been fortunate to experience some wondrous fishing in December, January and February, and I have taken dozens of fish on a single trip during the dog-days of summer, but those times are few.

With everything considered, there are no bad times to be on the flats in pursuit of bonefish. There are just better times.

This small, flowered park is located in New Plymouth, Green Turtle Cay, Bahamas.

FOOD AND FLIES

Bonefish are gluttons when it comes to what they will stuff down their bellies. These fish are considered opportunistic feeders and are known to utilize a smorgasbord of food. They always seem to be on the move hunting something to eat.

I have never killed a bonefish, so I cannot state firsthand what is apt to be found in their stomachs, but according to studies conducted in various parts of the Caribbean their diet includes just about anything—from crabs and mussels to shrimp and snails, to worms and miscellaneous small fish.

There are several important points to keep in mind when thinking about bonefish foods because they have a direct correlation on how we fish for them, and what type, size and color flies are used.

Of paramount importance is the fact that bonefish are bottom feeders. They will accept offerings suspended below the surface, even on the surface under the right conditions, but the vast majority of their foods are bottom dwellers and that is the place to fish for bones. It is vital that flies sink once they hit the water. It is the key factor when selecting flies.

But to tie on a large weighted fly simply because it hits the bottom quickly can be a major mistake. Whether a fly is weighted or not depends upon several factors, water depth being one. It only makes sense, the deeper the water the longer it takes to reach the bottom. If working areas knee deep a heavier fly than when working water just a few inches deep might be called for. A heavier fly might also be needed on a windy or blustery day, while a lighter fly is generally best on calm occasions. When wading and the wind is calm, an unweighted fly will generally do the trick, especially when there is sufficient time to pick out a target and make a cast, but when working from the bow of a skiff and quick casts might be necessary, flies that get to the bottom fast, are a big plus.

The bonefish hunter should carry both weighted and unweighted flies, since it is never known with absolute certainty

which type will be needed and because circumstances change from flat to flat, even tide to tide. It is also unknown what mood your adversary will be in, spooky and uncooperative or willing and forgiving. Heavy flies typically hit the water harder than unweighted flies, so if the fish is wary, or close casts might be called for, unweighted flies are the way to go.

If all else fails, cast as close to the bonefish as conditions allow, but never directly at it, the fly should be resting on the bottom when the fish arrives. Bonefish typically cruise and hunt a flat between one and three miles per hour so if you cast directly towards it not only is there a greater chance of spooking it but the fly will land behind it rather than in front. Sum up the situation, and then make your move taking into consideration the speed it is traveling, whether it is tailing or mudding, water depth and sink rate of the fly. Flies should reach bottom within two to three seconds of hitting the water, which means most should land six to 10-feet ahead of the fish.

The same goes for having a variety of flies in different sizes. Bonefish have small mouths, and consequently the natural foods they hunt are also small, most running from about an inch or slightly less to 2-1/2-inches long. If the angler knows the size of natural foods in the area, or what specifically is being eaten, matching the relative size of the natural is the best way to go. If not, throughout much of the Caribbean sizes 4 and 6 are generally the place to start and are most productive. In the Florida Keys these sizes are still good and very popular, but when the big bones arrive in Key Biscayne and other Key flats in April and May, larger sizes often produce best. The same is true on the east side of Bimini in the Bahamas in January.

The point is, flies of varying size should also be available, with some size 2 and size 8, but predominately size 4 and 6, unless larger and super small flies are specifically recommended prior to your trip. Keep in mind even the largest bonefish foods rarely exceed 2-1/2-inches, so neither should your flies. If you're unsure what to tie on and use first, don't hesitate to ask your guide. Just be prepared with a good size selection.

Another reason for having different size flies on hand is varying fishing conditions. Small (and unweighted) flies are nearly always best in shallow, clear water areas and when the surface is flat and the sky is bright since under these conditions bonefish have good visibility and small flies can be delivered with the least amount of disturbance, even when casting close to the target. Bigger offerings (and weighted) are generally the best way to go in

deeper water, when the water is clouded or the surface is broken, or on overcast days.

Keep in mind, however, while large and heavy flies have their place, and can actually save the day under some circumstances, they are harder to cast, and generally make more noise when they kiss the water. Unless the caster is adept at the craft, it is always dangerous to cast large offerings close to the target unless actively tailing. Even then there is always a danger. A general rule of thumb is to never drop any fly larger than size 4 closer than six-feet from the target. You might get away with a smaller fly providing it gets to the bottom quickly, but it is too much of a gamble with large, heavy flies.

Shape and color of bonefish flies are important factors as well. Bonefish fly development still has a long way to go, and presently

To successfully take bonefish, tarpon and permit, all hooks must be sharp. Hooks should be checked before use, and after each fish is caught.

the vast majority of the most popular designs resemble shrimp and crabs. The Ultra Shrimp, Mini Puff, Puff, Crazy Charlie, and various epoxy flies, to name a few, are prime shrimp examples. In general, sticking with shrimp and small crab imitations until additional flies are developed is about the only thing the angler can do, but that seems sufficient. They have worked for years and caught hundred of bones and will continue to do so.

I like to carry flies in a rainbow of colors. It is difficult to believe, but fly color can make all the difference in the world from one location of the Caribbean to the other, even from flat to flat and tide to tide. Jack Simpson, President, International Federation of Sport Fly Fishing swears offerings in brown, yellow and chartreuse are the only way to go in Cuba; but my Honduran guide, a knowledgeable youngster by the name of Carmen, insists on green offerings for waters around Guanaja Bay Island. Fishing companion Scott Heywood of Angling Destinations out of Sheridan, Wyoming, who spends considerable time in the Bahamas, likes flies in colors of orange, pink, chartreuse and tan. Color does make a difference!

This truism is based upon habitat conditions in a given area, varying light conditions at various tide levels and water depths and resident forage. Unless the visiting angler has been to a destination before, he or she really never knows what foods are dominant in an area, or what color they are, so selecting the right color fly is really a guess. The best route is to inquire before even leaving home and to stock up on colors (and sizes). Lodges, guides or booking agents specializing in angling travel generally have fly pattern information.

The other option, though more expensive unless you tie your own flies, is to amass a good selection in a wide array of colors and shades. Everything from tan and white to green and chartreuse. Keep in mind bonefish have acute color vision and can distinguish about 24 colors along a narrow band. Even if certain colored flies seem to work best in a given area or even on a certain flat, having an assortment of flies available in a variety of colors is not a bad idea. Supple, natural shades like tan, brown, olive and gold are always with me when I'm working the flats, but so are the brighter colors, orange, green, pink, white and yellow. In general, soft colors seem to work best under clear, bright skies, when water is shallow and clear. Darker, harsher colors seem to do best under cloudy conditions, in deep water, when water is murky or somewhat discolored, on a rising tide when bones are typically more aggressive and whenever light conditions are not intense.

Following is a list of popular bonefish flies known to work in the Caribbean. These and others are available at fly shops catering to the bonefish, tarpon and permit angler and by mail order from numerous outlets. A list of commercial sources will be found following "Part 3" of this book. Many fishing camps in the Caribbean also have a selection available for sale, but not all. Tying instructions for many can be found in such books as *Saltwater Flies: Over 700 of the Best* by Deke Meyer, *Flies for Saltwater* by Dick Stewart and Farrow Allen and *Bonefishing With A Fly* by Randall Kaufmann.

BONEFISH FLIES

Those followed by an **(*)** are available in various color combinations. Those in **bold face** are considered standards and are among the most popular bonefish flies.

Arbona's Shrimp	**Epoxy Charlie (*)**
Agent Bonefish	**Epoxy Puff (*)**
Agent Orange	Fernandez's Honey Shrimp
Bentback **(*)**	Florida Shrimp
Blind Charlie**(*)**	Frankee Belle
Bonefish Bugger **(*)**	Golden Mantis Shrimp
Bonefish Clouser **(*)**	**Horror**
Bonefish Critter **(*)**	**McCrab**
Bonefish Special	**Mini Puff**
Burel Translucent Minnow	**Mini Puff Epoxy**
Bimini Bone	Mother of Epoxy **(*)**
Bonnie's Evil Eye	Mercer's Transparent
Bearded Charlie	Moffo Dark Mohair Shrimp
Bonefish Gotcha	Nix's Epoxy Fly **(*)**
Canard Crab	**Puff**
Clouser Minnow (*)	**Pops Bonefish Bitters (*)**
Copper Liz	Rogers Shimmering Shrimp **(*)**
Crazy Charlie (*)	Son of Clouser
Crystal Charlie	T-Bone
Deepsalt Minnow **(*)**	Ultra Shrimp
Diamond Epoxy	Winston's Urchins **(*)**
Diamond Halfback	Yucatan Charlie

SPOTTING BONEFISH

One of the greatest challenges for the novice bonefish enthusiast is spotting these silver demons on the flats. I have been hunting bonefish for years now, and though my ability to detect activity and their presence is getting better each time out, no matter how carefully I work a flat and force my eyes to detect fish there are still times and conditions when I just can't see them! At times it is frustrating, and I envy the person who has developed the ability and skill to spot these fish even when there seems to be none around.

In *Bonefishing with a Fly*, Randall Kaufmann writes, "Spotting bonefish is a skill of perception rather than acuity"… "Anglers seldom see a well defined bonefish, but are looking for anything out of the ordinary, specifically motions, wakes, tails, color contrast, often fish themselves. Often an ill-defined shape or shadow, blurred movement or subtle surface disturbance will alert you to concentrate on a particular area, which hopefully will reveal the object of your search."

Looking back, I can honestly say there have been few instances when I actually detected a bonefish prior to some tell-tale sign of its presence. Even after countless hours on the flats I have yet to develop the ability of seeing fish without some kind of sign. My particular problem is most acute while wading, where the fisherman's angle of view is greatly reduced and reflection of sun and clouds off the water is more enhanced. Working from the bow of a flats skiff presents far less of a problem and my spotting ratio is far greater. The advantage of being several feet above the water provides a larger downward angle of view, and in many cases sun reflection is less of a problem. For these reasons, the novice bonefish hunter or those having difficulty spotting fish while wading might want to hone their skills from a skiff first.

But even then spotting bonefish remains a challenge. Bonefish have the ability to change color, or take on the same color of the environment surrounding them. On light sandy bottoms they may appear silver, but on bottoms with turtle grass or coral they may appear dark or mottled. Sunlight, clouds, clarity of water and water depth, and wind all play a roll in the angler's spotting ability, and each scenario is different, even different times of day and different times of tide. Things keep changing on the flats, and in order to be successful the angler must be able to adapt and spot bonefish as those changes present themselves.

Eventually it becomes easier to spot bonefish under varying conditions. When that will happen is relative, depending upon how astute the student and how much time is spent on the flats, but in the beginning it soon becomes obvious which conditions offer the best chances of spotting fish on a personal basis. Personally, I find it doesn't get any easier than in shallow water on a rising tide, when the sun is directly overhead under a clear sky accompanied by a gentle breeze. Spotting fish is generally easier when the water is shallow, but when the tide is inbound and fresh fish are moving onto a flat from deep areas they seem to be darker along the backs making them stand out better.

When the sun is at its daytime high, or for perhaps an hour or two on either side, the greatest amount of light is directly on the back of the fish which greatly minimizes shadows and reflection, again making them easier to spot. It is also much easier to see the bottom during these hours, and therefore fish as well.

Again, which scenario is best for you is relative. But keep in mind "ideal" conditions are not present all the time. In fact, chances are they rarely will be, so it is vital to master the art of spotting under varying conditions.

So the question remains, what do you look for? While fishing the Crooked Island area in the Bahamas recently, I popped that question to Scott Heywood who spent some of his childhood in that area and who I swear can spot bonefish in a dark closet. His reply was quite simple and to the point.

"Most anglers commit the mistake of looking at the water, like they would trout rising to the surface; instead look through the water and at the bottom. It takes some adjustment and getting used to, but if you train yourself to look below the surface for moving shadows, off color shapes or forms, or any sudden flashes of silver, spotting these fish becomes a lot easier."

Captain Tony Traad, a tarpon specialist who works Biscayne Bay, the Everglades and upper Keys agrees. "You have to forget everything you know about trout and salmon," Traad says. "These fish are near the bottom—because that's where their feed is—and unless tailing, are always on the move. So look for movement close to the bottom not on top."

Of course, as many bonefish hunters soon learn, training the eye to concentrate below the surface is easier said than done, but when stalking the flats it is primary to success. I have discovered, however, something else is important as well: Don't bite off more than you can chew.

Depending upon skill, anglers are able to spot bonefish at various distances. For some it may be as little as 15 feet, for others perhaps up to 50 or 60 feet. Whatever the distance, the bottom and just about everything on it is clearly visible. This is known as the "concentration" or "pick-up" zone as I call it, and it quickly becomes apparent what your maximum range is. Your ability to spot fish at longer distances may vary depending upon conditions, and whether fishing from a boat or wading, but the important thing is this is the maximum extent your eyes can detect fish and it should not be extended until further training allows you to do so. A main problem with many bonefish enthusiasts, particularly those just starting out with few hours on the flats, is that they try to cover too much area too soon. They scan too far away, can't see fish, spook those close at hand, get frustrated and therefore see and catch far less fish.

It is much easier, and more productive for the learning eye to concentrate closer in, occasionally looking beyond that point for any tailing fish or fish providing obvious signs of their whereabouts. When wading I consider my maximum "pick-up" zone to be about 20 to 25 feet, or 35 to 40 feet from a flats boat, but it is sometimes much less or greater depending upon light conditions, water depth and other factors. The

maximum range of other anglers may be much greater, but I know my limits and that is the area that gets nearly all my attention.

Other things to be watchful for are classic indicators bonefish are in the area, particularly "V" water, nervous water and fish that may be tailing. Here again, these signs are always easy to detect, especially when the surface is rippled, which is a great deal of the time, but they eventually become more apparent and easy to note.

"V" water is created by tails and/or dorsal fins when bonefish are on the move and is generally most obvious in shallow-water areas where the bottom is a foot to 15 inches below the surface. However, it is also a phenomenon in slightly deeper water, perhaps up to 20 inches or so, so it is something I am always watchful of whenever on the flats in water below the knee. In the majority of cases neither tail nor dorsal fin is visible to the eye, but in water that is heavily rippled the wake they create, which resembles a number of torpedoes coming your way, is quite obvious, particularly if it happens to be a school of fish rather than a single one. The "V" water created by a lone fish is much more difficult to observe.

Nervous water is another telltale sign of bonefish, and is generally the result of fish movement—particularly schools of bonefish—in deeper water. It is basically created by the school pushing water as they advance which leaves an out-of-place rippling action on the surface which seems to move against the tide or current, is out-of-color or is otherwise at odds with the surrounding area. Nervous water is easiest to detect on a flat surface, but even when rippled by wind or tide, can be easier to detect than "V" water.   Of the various signs which typically suggest bonefish are in your area, seeing tailing fish is the one which thrills me most. Not only is seeing a tail protruding from the water an obvious "here I am" sign, it is an exciting and adrenaline-pumping vision few other things on the flats can equal.

When bonefish feed, they tip downward which sends the tail, and sometimes the dorsal fin as well, upward and often above the surface of the water, depending upon water depth. This is called "tailing," and in shallow water or when the light conditions are just right it is possible to easily note their whereabouts when in this feeding mode. At times, however, when the sun is bright and reflecting off the surface tailing bonefish can be camouflaged by the rippling action on the water. Knowing that, it is to the angler's advantage to keep in mind bonefish often rock from side to side as they root food off the bottom, sometimes rather vigorously, making a noticeable disturbance in the process. Because of that fact not only is it necessary to look carefully for a tail extending above the surface, but it is equally as important to look for this back-and-forth motion as well. On bright days when the sun is extreme or other conditions make spotting a challenge, it is often this agitating motion which first draws the human eye and makes the presence of bonefish known. But don't forget that tail and dorsal fin waving back and forth. During this feeding procedure the dorsal fin

will also make a slight splashing sound as it moves from side to side against the water. This soft, almost delicate vibration can often be heard above the sound of the rippling water and wind, making your ears as important as your eyes.

Another favorite sign of mine, because it is so obvious in a good many situations, is a "mud." This is basically an area where bonefish are either actively feeding or have been recently feeding, and have stirred up the bottom creating a cloud of discolored water. From the bow of a boat large muds are quite noticeable, less so while wading, but for the novice muds created by a school of fish are one of the easiest signs to discern and recognize as an area where bonefish are either present or have been recently active. Muds are typically an area of murky, grayish off-colored water which seems to be hanging just below the surface.

If a mud is active it can also be quite easy and forgiving to fish, and bones working the area are often aggressive because of the feeding frenzy in progress. The discolored water helps obscure the delivery of flies and any ill-placed presentations. An active mud can be a welcome gift to the novice but less exciting to those more schooled in the art of spotting bonefish on the flats. I have fished muds in Belize, the Bahamas and other spots in the Caribbean basin where fish after fish were caught bordering on the unexciting. Some might even claim working an active mud can be rather boring, and at times I would agree. But a bonefish is a bonefish is a bonefish. And I rarely pass up the opportunity, figuring it is one of God's little blessings, a payback if you will, for all those fish I missed or didn't happen to spot under different circumstances.

There are a couple things to remember about muds, however. Other visitors to the flats create them as well, rays and permit to name two, and it can be difficult to determine their true origin unless bonefish are actually observed. A disturbed bottom can also remain cloudy long after bonefish have departed the area. Fresh muds are generally darker, thicker looking and appear more dense, while older muds are just the opposite. Whatever the case may be, all muds deserve a careful approach. Even if a mud is fresh and bonefish are working the area and their visibility may be restricted they are still highly susceptible to noise so take it slow. This is true in mud areas where activity seems to have tapered off. Vacated muds often attract other bonefish cruising or traveling through an area, and a number of fish or a lone monster may linger behind for leftover tidbits, again, necessitating a slow, careful, quiet and tactful approach.

Parrots and other tropical birds await visitors to Posada del Sol.

Working at a snail's pace and quietly on the flats cannot be over emphasized. If any of the senses bonefish possess matches their vision it is their ability to hear. There have been occasions when I swear they could hear the wind kissing the water surface. Whether this is true or not I honestly cannot say, but their ability to hear sound is acute, so it is to the angler's advantage to always work slow and not make noise either in a boat or wading. When doing the latter, if the angler can hear himself pushing water or hear water rippling past his legs as he moves, it has been my experience he is working too fast. Slow down. Not only is it much quieter and fewer fish spooked, but it provides more time to carefully scrutinize the water and flat being fished.

Whether fishing from a boat or wading it is always a major asset to have the sun at your back, or at least off to one side. This not only greatly increases angler visibility, but forces bonefish to look into it which slightly deters their ability to detect your presence. It is also best to work in the same direction as the tide. Bonefish typically feed against the tide, which means when the angler sees them they will be coming towards him head on or off to one side, the two best casting angles.

And finally, always watch for shadows or silhouettes being cast on the water, either that of your person, or from your fly rod or line, and try to maintain a low profile, whenever working a flat. This is true for bonefish, but also for permit and in many cases for tarpon as well. Next to noise, lines flying overhead and sending off glare, flies slapping the water and shadows cast by anglers and their equipment are what spook bonefish most.

Because these fish are generally found in shallow water, bright light and clear water conditions, bonefish have a generous window of observation and it is always best to reduce that window whenever possible. If the fish are 40 or 50 feet away it may not be quite as necessary, but when under 40 feet out and casting from a skiff I generally cast on my knees knowing the higher and closer to the fish I am the better the chance of being seen. When wading and the fish are close it is not unusual for me to cast from a bending position or even on my knees with water up to my waist.

Each situation is different and at times it may not be necessary to go to such an extreme. Casting from a bending or even standing position will suffice, but the condition will dictate what is needed and as experience is obtained the angler will automatically know. Whether standing, bending or on your knees, be prepared to cast from these positions. Learn how to before heading for the flats.

CASTING AND THE RETRIEVE

One of the great challenges when casting to bonefish is that they are nearly always on the move which dictates casting to a non-stationary target. This can be a great deal of fun, but in most cases it is a test of one's ability to get a fly to a selected position quickly, accurately and without disturbing the water or notifying the fish of your whereabouts.

Because conditions on a flat change from day to day, tide to tide, hour to hour, even from fish to fish each situation is different and there are a number of rules which must be adhered to.

As just indicated working from a bending or kneeling position is one, but keep in mind bonefish are always on the move, and frequently change direction on their seemingly haphazard search for food. Because of this fact being able to cast quickly in any direction is a major plus, and that means casting with, against or across wind. Having the wind at your back, or coming to your side and casting with or across wind should also be a first choice, but if the situation dictates otherwise, be prepared to handle it. Knowing how to cast a tight loop helps maintain control, increases accuracy and line speed allowing for quick delivery, and helps cut the wind.

Also important is being able to cast 30 to 40 feet quickly and with accuracy. Being able to quickly cast greater distances, 50

feet or more, and still possess the ability to put your fly where you want it is even better, but about a dozen yards is minimum in most bonefish situations. For most casters, the closer a cruising bonefish or school of bones gets, the chance of making a cast and dropping a fly and causing alarm increases. Experienced stalkers and casters often get within a few feet with success, most even prefer it and make a game out of doing so, but 30 to 40 feet is a safe distance in most cases. A good rule of thumb I adhere to is never let your cruising target get too close, and I let that little voice inside and knowledge of my ability be the judge. If conditions allow I will make an 80 or 90 foot cast. I prefer a cast between 60 and 70 feet because I am much more accurate at that distance yet it still allows an opportunity for a second attempt if my offering is passed by, but rarely will I cast to moving fish closer than 30 feet. The chances of spooking the school are just too great, and I'd just as soon wait for a better opportunity.

The exception to this rule is when I spot a tailing bonefish, or several tailers, dutifully rooting food off the bottom. In this scenario it is often best, as well as a personal challenge, to sneak within just a few feet and make a cast. Long lengths of line, along with leader and fly, not only require accelerated line speed to stay in the air but are more difficult to control and deliver accurately for many casters, and typically hit the water

Locating bonefish on the flats is a challenging endeavor. Here the author has some difficulty, and his guide, Carmen helps him out. The key is to look through the water at the bottom, not on the surface.

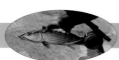

harder than short casts, thus increasing the chances of alarming fish. If your target is tailing, sneak in as close as possible, or to whatever distance feels right, before making your cast. But keep in mind, that everything from the cast and dropping the fly to the retrieve has to be near perfect, and the best you can hope for is perhaps one or two attempts.

Equally as important is proper placement of your fly, and getting it in position quickly. Remember, unless the fish you see are tailing and concentrated on one specific area they will be moving, and though they may appear not to be traveling fast, bonefish cover a great deal of ground quickly. Because of this two things are rather important. Always be prepared and have your rod and line ready to cast on a moment's notice, and have your fly on the bottom and ready to retrieve before the target comes into range.

The first can be achieved rather easily. While in the process of wading, the rod is held in the casting hand with the tip pointing slightly upward but off to the side or slightly backwards. The fly is held between the thumb and first finger. At least 15 to 20 feet of line should extend past the rod tip and be allowed to tag along behind you on the surface. Experienced casters often have 20 to 25 feet of line past the tip. When ready to cast simply make a swift forward or roll-type cast to get the line moving at which point two things can be done. You can hold on to the fly as the line comes forward, which many claim helps load the rod, releasing the fly on the back cast, or you can release the fly on the initial cast forward, make a backcast and then shoot to the target. If the target is further away than the length of line extending past the rod tip, which is often the case, it may be necessary to extend the length of the line on a second or even third forward cast.

But the key here is to make as few casts as possible thus reducing the chance of spooking the fish, and getting the fly in the water as soon as possible. For the average caster if more than two of three forward casts are needed to reach the mark, the fish is simply too far away. The same basic procedure is used when fishing from a boat. However, instead of having line in the water it should be coiled neatly at your feet on the deck and ready to shoot. The caution here, particularly during long intervals between fish, is that you don't step on the line or otherwise tangle it. Check it periodically, and make sure it doesn't get wrapped around any gear, anchor ropes and mooring ties.

Typically, there are two ways to cast to bonefish, the traditional overhead cast or casting with the rod low and off to the side. The same is true of permit and tarpon, and which to use depends on two things; what the angler can perform best and the circumstances at the time.

The overhead cast is easier for most, but there is the threat of scaring fish with the line and delivering the fly too hard to the water, especially when fish are close. This cast is best used when the target is more than 40 or 50 feet away when wading, 50 to 60 feet away when casting from a boat and wind is not a contributing factor. Even then there is the danger of slapping the water with line and fly, so to help lessen the threat cast to and stop

your final cast at an imaginary mark four to five feet above the water. By doing so the line will straighten out and lose its energy above the water, and drop to the surface much more gently.

Whenever possible, however, particularly when fish are in close and wind is playing a role, the side arm cast should be used. I use it almost exclusively when casting to bonefish and permit, even tarpon when in close, and believe it plays a major role in successfully getting the fly to the target area without spooking fish.

In a majority of cases it is best to maintain a low cast, keeping the fly line and any shadow or reflection it may create near the water where it is less apt to be detected. Because the line is much closer to the water with this cast, the line and fly also drop to the surface with less disturbance, again reducing the chances of spooking fish. And when casting into the wind, or on windswept days in general, the side-arm cast makes casting easier and is much more accurate.

Fly presentation to feeding or cruising bonefish is critical. The biggest mistake committed by novice enthusiasts when casting, and at times by more experienced participants, is casting directly to the fish, or misjudging the distance and casting over the fish or dropping the fly too close. This is a big no-no and invariably results in either dropping the fly behind the fish where it can't be seen or alarming your target and spooking them.

While it is always best to get your fly as close as possible, keep in mind several factors: wind, water depth and how fast fish are moving or not moving. There are many variables which dictate how a fly should be presented. I discovered early on how each situation should be handled—whether fish are coming directly at you, off to the side, going away; whether it is a school of fish or a lone giant off by itself, whether fish are tailing or cruising in deep water or shallow, in a heavy wind or no wind—experience and trial and error is the best teacher.

It is a truism that no matter how much you read, or how many hours a guide spends trying to instruct you, nothing is more instructive or imprints deeper into the brain than learning something firsthand. Books, videos and guides may get you pointed in the right direction, but like anything else in life, whether an angler gets to be good on the flats for bonefish, permit or tarpon depends on how much time and effort is invested in the pursuit. If heading to the flats for the first time, or if you have little experience go with the attitude that it is a learning experience. It always will be. Accept the fact you will make mistakes. If you catch fish, fine. But if you don't that is okay, too. We all started out somewhere. None of us were born experts, and what makes these fish so addictive is they do make all of us look foolish from time to time no matter how good we think we are. The important thing is learn, have fun, enjoy being on the flats and accept the fact that while it won't come easy, it will come.

In a majority of cases how the fly should be delivered generally falls in one of two broad categories. The first is to drop your fly close enough so it will be seen, but not so close it will cause

bonefish to flee the area. This is often the best approach when bonefish are actively tailing or creating a mud or when encountering cruising fish. You want to draw their attention with the fly. In either scenario, it is always a risk to drop a fly closer than three to five feet from the fish, depending upon the situation. It is sometimes possible to do so, but it is always a risk. Also, when casting to tailing bonefish, always remember to time your cast so the fly hits the water when the fish is tipped downward or is rocking back and forth and has its mind on food. Their vision is not as acute at this time, greatly reducing the chances of it seeing you, the fly line or noticing the fly as it hits the water.

The second casting technique is to drop the fly across the intended path of moving fish so it can be worked into view and intercepted as they pass. The important thing to remember is to note the direction and speed of the fish, getting into proper casting position and not deliver the fly too soon. I like to cast slightly off to one side since it keeps the fish parallel to me rather than coming head on, and ideally I like to have my fly either coming to rest or fully resting on the bottom for no more than five or six seconds before I start my retrieve. If the fly rests on the bottom longer than that, there is a chance the fish may change direction forcing me to lift the fly and make another cast, something I don't want to do.

Many bonefishermen don't think so, but I happen to believe the way a fly is retrieved is nearly as important as the cast. Of course, any retrieve is a waste of time if a poor cast is made, or if the fish can't see the fly. But by the same token just because the fly is seen doesn't automatically mean a bonefish, or any fish for that matter, will move in and nail it. The way a fly is worked has a great deal to do with the way a fish responds to that fly.

Properly retrieving a bonefish fly is not that difficult. The main objective is to get the fly in view of the fish, and work it in such a manner that will not only draw attention but create enough excitement to induce a strike. Sometimes this is easier said than done, but once the cast has been successfully made, the rest is generally not that difficult.

Upon completing the cast, regardless of whether fishing from a boat or wading, the rod tip should be pointed directly at the target and slanted downward towards the water. In fact, having the rod tip an inch or so below the surface is not a bad idea, but the important thing is to fish a slack-free line. This not only allows better command and control of the fly, but allows the angler to "feel" the slightest amount of resistance in the event of a strike. Furthermore, if the fly is refused, or if the target begins to swim away, additional action will need to be applied and it is much easier to do so with a tight line. The fly line is placed under the index finger of your rod hand, and line is stripped by pulling with your free hand.

The strip itself is basically nothing more than a series of pulls on the line, which in turn moves the fly. A combination of fast, slow, short, long strips broken by occasional stops can be employed, and which combination is best is generally dictated by the response of the fish, and to a certain degree by water

Dr. Ron Apter scans the marl for bonefish. "Doc", managed to take a dozen or so bones during our day in the area.

depth. The important thing to keep in mind is that natural foods which bonefish eat move at a relatively slow pace, so a "snail's pace," moving the fly just a couple inches on each strip, is a good place to start once the fly is in proper position. At times, for example when a fish is actively tailing, not moving the fly any distance but with a few quick twitches forcing it to move in an up and down fashion to draw attention is the best way to go. When little interest in the fly is indicated, a faster, longer strip might turn the fish on. Here again, just like casting, each scenario is different, and it is up to the angler to determine which retrieve method should be employed.

Keep in mind, too, the longer a fly goes unobserved the more your chances for a strike diminish. It is generally best to strip the fly three or four times, stop, strip three or four more times, stop and then a third time, with each stop or pause lasting several seconds. If nothing happens, it might be more productive to gently retrieve the fly and make another cast.

HOOKING
AND PLAYING BONES

I compare bonefishing to fishing with nymphs. Many of the same subtleties and much of the same tact is employed, and though I have never tested the theory, I have no doubt the experienced nympher hitting the flats for the first time has an edge over the angler who has little or no experience with nymph imitations.

When a bonefish sets its sights on a fly and has made the mental decision to strike, it can come generally in one or two ways; soft and hardly noticeable, perhaps with only a slight hesitation or delicate tug on the fly, or rather aggressively, with determination and purpose. Whatever the case, the reel will

either begin to sing almost immediately or there will be a slight delay, almost as if the fish doesn't know it's been hooked. Because it is not known which event will take place, it is imperative the fly line is clear and able to run free and the drag is properly set beforehand.

Many novice enthusiasts set the drag too hard or not hard enough, generally the former. It helps to keep in mind once the initial run is on there is no way to actually stop these fish. Even on subsequent runs it can be difficult, so don't try, at least until the fish starts to tire. Constant pressure is always desired, so set drags with sufficient tension to help slow the blazing runs and keep pressure on the fish, but not so hard the leader will break; about one to two pounds pressure should be more than enough. Additional pressure can be increased as needed, either by adjusting the drag, raising the rod top or moving the rod to the left or right and adding side pressure.

Another common mistake is setting the hook prematurely by suddenly raising the rod tip. If you feel the fish, or believe the fly has been accepted, keep the rod level with the water with tip pointed at the fish and make a short but quick strip on the line. This will either set the hook, in which case the game is on, or it will slightly move the fly keeping it on or close to the bottom, in which case nothing is lost. Quickly raising the rod tip to set the hook will either spook any fish in the vicinity or remove the fly from the target area, or both.

Once the fish is on, it is testing fate to try and stop the run. Instead, enjoy it. After making sure the hook is firmly set, generally by slightly raising the rod tip, most anglers lift the rod, sending the tip skyward, but there is a threat of putting way too much pressure on the fish by doing this. Not only is drag supplied by the reel, which should be sufficient enough to add pressure and maintain control itself, but added pressure provided by the bend in the rod, plus increasing pressure as more line comes in contact with the water. This is a great deal of pressure on a fish blazing across the flats at several feet per second!

If this tactic works stick with it. But I prefer to let the reel do all the work and keep the tip lowered and pointed directly at the fish, particularly on the initial and second runs, when bonefish are full of spit and fire. I do the same for tarpon and permit. I know I can't stop the fish anyway, and by keeping the rod level with the water I know exactly how much pressure I have on my adversary. I also know as line is pulled off the reel increased pressure is being added as more line hits the water. Equally as important, however, the rod is not up in the air bouncing back and forth jerking and tugging on the leader and fly.

Never have the rod pointed at the fish when reeling in line or when trying to play or subdue the fish, or when fish are on runs when all the angler can do is hold on and marvel at it all. When the run is over, or when I want to retrieve line, I raise the rod which provides increased pressure while maintaining a slack-free line, and play the fish in the customary fashion, reeling downward to retrieve line and then pumping back. Depending upon the fish, side pressure may be added to maximize pressure.

Playing bonefish is the ultimate thrill and challenge to one's skills with a fly rod, but so is maintaining some kind of handling control as they near the boat or when the fish get in close when wading. Unless completely spent, bonefish seldom give up the fight, either circling, making short runs or splashing about trying to get free. Keep in mind it is always best to play any fish as quickly as possible to reduce stress and increase its chance of surviving. After two, three or four blazing runs much of the fun is over so apply maximum pressure by reigning the rod tip or applying side pressure and get that fish in! A good way to break the fish, especially when in close is to lift the head out of the water. This simply throws them off balance, takes away a lot of the fight and makes them easier to handle.

As the fish gets closer, keep your rod tip high, draw it closer and at the appropriate time, slide your hand down the leader and, keeping the fish in the water, remove the hook. If it is necessary to lift the fish from the water if photographs are desired, do so with wet hands. Turning the fish over on its back and holding it close to the body will help quiet it, and for picture taking, make sure to keep fingers away from the gills and eyes by gently grasping the fish around the back of the head and tail.

Dr. Craig Johnston plays a bonefish near Crooked Island, Bahamas. Bonefish, balmy breezes and warm sun is what the Bahamas are all about.

EQUIPMENT
Rods

I enjoy working the flats for bonefish with fly fishing outfits from size 5 up to 8 or 9. Permit typically demand gear on the heavy end of this range, tarpon even heavier gear, but bonefish offer a choice. Personally, I prefer to hunt these fish with the lightest kit possible but I am not always allowed to do so. Wind determines what size outfit is best on the flats, as does the size of fly being used and size of fish expected to be caught.

With everything considered, a 9 or 9-1/2 foot rod designed for number 8 line is for most anglers perhaps the best rig for bonefish. This size is not difficult to cast for long periods, it can handle wind up to the point where if it was blowing any harder you probably wouldn't be fishing, it can throw the largest of bonefish flies plus it can be delivered to the water with a minimum of disturbance under most conditions. On calm days especially, but also in extreme shallow water or when the fish are unusually nervous and shy, a lighter line will drop to the water more gently, so it is always a good idea to have two outfits. This is true not only because of varying conditions, but in case one is broken. It is a long hike between tackle stores in the Caribbean, so go prepared. It is also a wise idea to have an extra reel and line.

I generally travel with a size 6 and size 8 outfit, both ninefooters. The lighter of the two is used whenever possible, simply because I prefer it and find it more enjoyable to take bones on light tackle, but if the wind kicks up I have the heavier 8 weight to fall back on. Size 7 is a good middle of the road selection, but it is still on the light side on wind-swept days. A size 9, although used by some, is a bit heavy except on those days when casting something lighter is difficult or just not possible.

One thing I want in my rods, regardless of length, whether it be for bones, tarpon or permit is backbone and quickness. One of the keys to successfully fishing for these fish is being able to get the fly to the target area in a hurry, and this is a lot easier to do with a rod with a fast tip. I also like a rod that allows me to put some pressure on the fish, and a rod that refuses to bounce uncontrollably when line is being stripped off the reel. I also like three or four-piece pack rods, and always make sure my rod I take stays with me. Keep in mind that you will be flying, and though I have had my gear arrive late only once on numerous trips, it is a frustrating and unnerving circumstance that can cut a day or two off your trip. The airlines do a good job, but baggage does get lost or arrive late on occasion. Keep a small carry-on pack loaded with a reel, flies, leaders and other paraphernalia along with a change of clothes and some personal items with you, along with your rod.

As for reels, any single action reel with a reliable, smooth drag and capable of holding at least 150-yards of 25 to 30-pound test backing will handle most bonefish. Large bones have been known to strip out more than that, so 200 yards of backing is not unreasonable.

Along with sufficient backing, the important thing is that your reel releases line smoothly when the drag is set. If the reel skips or chatters when the fish is screaming across the flats something is going to give, and chances are it will be the tippet. Drag adjustment buttons should also be large and easy to locate, allowing the angler to make quick settings without searching for, and fighting with, the adjustment.

Reels

Of the various fly reel designs available, however, the anti-reverse is my favorite. I have been using the STH Caribbean or Valentine Planetary Model 350 reels for years on bones, permit and small tarpon and swear by the anti-reverse design. The Valentine is not an anti-reverse in the purest sense; only the rewind handle turns as line is being stripped while the spool remains stationary. But the important thing is the anti-reverse design allows the angler to keep the hand used to retrieve line on the reel at all times, even when line is going out. This eliminates the threat of placing a hand on the reel at an inappropriate time which may break the fish off or damage fingers and knuckles, and ultimately, because your hand is already on the reel helps speed up the process of retrieving line. Both reels also meet the criteria I look for in a fly reel, adequate line capacity, smooth, reliable, strong drags and dependability. As recommended with fly rods, take two reels on any trip, just in case, and an extra spool of line and backing as well.

The author scans a flat in south Florida for bonefish. Notice the fly in his free hand, and line dropping from his rod hand and reel ready to cast. This is the proper way to hunt bonefish, permit and tarpon from the bow of a flats skiff.

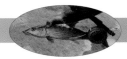

A bonefish about to be released by the author. The reel is a Valentince Planetary, one of the authors favorites, and a perfect match for bonefish throughout the Caribbean.

Lines

Many fly fishermen don't put much emphasis on fly line selection, giving more thought to rod and reel instead. The truth of the matter is the right fly line is important for proper casting technique, particularly into the wind and in the heat of the tropics.

Water temperatures in bonefish country generally exceed 80-degrees F. Such temperatures heat a fly line making them soft, limp and overly supple in the process which not only makes them less responsive to angler demands but more difficult to cast thus effecting delivery and presentation. Lines get even warmer while resting on the deck of a boat. Because of this fact I like a line that is less heat sensitive, a line that will remain somewhat stiff even under intense sun and heat.

Not all lines meet this criteria, but the 444SL Saltwater lines by Cortland do, and I use them almost exclusively when on the flats, not just for bones but for permit and tarpon as well. In fact these lines were specifically engineered and designed with this problem in mind. The Orvis Tropic Fly Lines are good, too. Other lines will work, of course. Even the lines generally used in freshwater for salmon, trout and steelhead. But if you intend to spend any amount of time in the Caribbean, one of these specialty lines created specifically for warm water will perform far better.

As is well-known, fly lines are available in various tapers and densities, but the weight-forward floater is the standard. Here again, the specialty lines offer some advantages. Cortland's 444SL Bonefish Taper, for example, has a longer front taper and body which not only helps make delivery more delicate but reduces the amount of line that has to be stripped in before picking up and re-casting, a major plus when casting to cruising fish.

One other thing about fly lines. When loading your fly reel, take some kind of felt marker, like a Magic Marker, in black or fluorescent orange or pink, and color-code in 10-foot sections the first 100 feet of backing on the reel. In other words, 10-feet colored, 10-feet white, 10-feet colored and so on. The same with your permit and tarpon reels, except for the latter I generally color-code the first 150 feet. These fish strip out a tremendous amount of line at blazing speed. When this color-coded line appears you will know how much line remains on the reel and can then take the necessary measures.

Leaders

Leaders are extremely important, too. In fact when it comes to bonefish, permit and tarpon the leader is a key factor governing success. Although bonefish seem to be more fly line shy than leader shy, the average leader is in the neighborhood of 10 to 12

feet, perhaps even 14 feet, depending upon conditions. If unaccustomed to working with long leaders a good length to start with is the same length as your rod, 9 to 9-1/2 feet. This is my preferred leader length, only under extreme wind conditions should bonefish leaders be shorter. For most situations a leader of 9 to 10 feet is just fine, but be prepared to go longer if it is a calm, windless day and the surface is mirror flat. It will make a difference.

Bonefish leaders should also be tapered. If you happen to be into constructing your own fine, but I prefer to catch fish and dislike making leaders with a passion. I have been using the commercially available systems offered by Umpqua, Climax and others with great success since I first started fishing the flats and I see no reason to change now. Leaders with a tippet in the eight or 10-pound test class will help land fish quicker and with less chance of a break-off, particularly for the novice, but here again, on a flat surface or when fish are overly spooky a six-pound test tippet might be called for. Go prepared with a good supply of leaders in various lengths and tippet sizes, and take plenty of tippet material as well. As for connecting leaders to the fly line, whether it be for bonefish, permit or tarpon, nothing beats the loop-to-loop system. Use either a whipped-loop directly in the end of the fly line, which is best, especially for tarpon and permit, or a permanent piece of 25-pound test monofilament attached to the fly line with a nail knot or needle nail knot and a loop in the other end. It is fast, easy and strong.

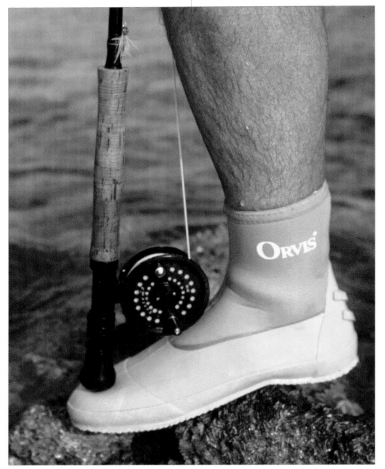

The flats are a maze of coral, turtle grass, soft marl, sand and other hidden objects. Proper foot gear is vital for comfort and safety.

Knots

Something else about knots. You don't have to be a wizard at constructing knots to catch bonefish. If using the loop-to-loop system, once backing and fly line is on the reel, which can often be done at a fly or tackle shop upon request, or quite easily done at home or at a fishing camp, using an arbor knot for backing to reel and nail knot to attach fly line to backing, about the only knots to be concerned with are the improved clinch knot, for attaching fly to leader, the simple blood knot for attaching tippet material to the tag end of a leader, and the nail knot for attaching new backing to a new fly line, in case the need should arise. Of course, it doesn't hurt to know how to construct a whipped loop in the end of a fly line, and have the tools along to do so. But in an emergency, simply stripping off two- inches of plastic coating on the end of a fly line and creating a single over-hand knot forming a loop will get you through.

Sunglasses

Other equipment is needed when fishing the flats, regardless of the target, that is just as important as fly rod, reel, lines, leaders and flies.

For the eyes, sunglasses are a must. It is next to impossible to fish under the glaring tropical sun without them, plus there is a danger of damaging the eyes if you don't wear them. Sunglasses are also a much needed spotting device that allow the angler to see through the glare and reflection and observe fish.

It is important to purchase the right sunglasses. There are a lot of glasses available at the local pharmacy or department store, but you couldn't pay me enough to wear them on the flats. Look for names like Bausch & Lomb, Nikon, Ray-Ban, Costa Del Mar and DAGS. All are top names and will serve you well.

Make sure sunglasses are polarized to reduce glare and sun reflection and that they provide ultraviolet or UV light protection. It is also a plus if they heighten perception, are distortion free and restrict the amount of sun reflecting back into the eyes by using an anti-reflective coating on the inside of the lens. Many don't. I also like my sunglasses to be light, the frames made of light metal, plastic or carbon, the lens made of a high quality plastic rather than glass. Make sure your glasses fit properly and cover as much of the eye area as possible. As for color amber and brown seem to be most popular on the flats.

A couple of other notes on eye protection. Glasses with side

shields are an added plus, as is a hanger strap. High quality sunglasses are expensive, and chances are you'll have only one pair with you, so keep them strapped around your neck.

Footwear

The Caribbean is blessed with magnificent white sand beaches and flats that are pure heaven to wade, but coral, razor sharp shells, spiny sea urchins, rays and other nasty critters and objects can slice, tear and enter the skin causing pain, discomfort and infection. Be prepared with good foot gear and be careful.

Learn how to walk a flat safely. Many flat enthusiasts say to lift your feet out of the water with each step, and then to angle them back into the water toe first. This is intended to minimize noise and reduce bottom disturbance, but also for safety. Except in extreme shallow water, where this tactic is best, I rarely feel comfortable repeatedly lifting my feet more than a few inches. Instead, in water higher than the ankle I merely lift each step two or three inches, keeping most of the foot below the surface, then gently placing it on the bottom, making sure of what is underneath before putting my full weight down. I have found it is just as quiet and, if moving at the speed I should, it is no more disturbing to the bottom, plus it allows me to feel and move around or move out of the way anything that might be underfoot. Move slow.

Wear the right foot gear. Even with careful wading there is always the chance of something coming in contact with the foot. You need protection. There are a number of wading boots offered by Orvis and others specifically designed for the flats. The tops are generally made of neoprene for comfort, a tight fit and fast drying, while the bottoms are hard rubber, sometimes with an interior felt midsole for added support and to prevent penetration by coral and other objects. Such boots are also extremely light, and can be worn all day with ease. I even wear them while working from the bow of a boat.

If primarily fishing from a boat, however, a simple pair of neoprene slippers or booties is even better. You might want nothing at all. I often go barefoot, but even in a boat there is danger and after hours under a tropical sun even the deck of a boat can get unbearably hot.

First Aid Kit

And finally, have a small first aid kit with you at all times. The kit should include a pair of tweezers in case you have to remove a piece of coral or urchin spine, some antiseptic liquid or cream such as Cortisone or hydrogen peroxide solution, Q-tips or cotton swabs and Band-Aids.

Clothing

Give your clothing some thought, too. You will be under the hot sun for hours on end and there is always the threat of a rain shower or outright downpour. You want clothes that are comfortable, offer protection from the sun, clothing that "breathes" and

provides air circulation, and clothes that dry quickly. The new synthetic materials or synthetics blended with cotton such as those offered by Tarponwear and Ex-Officio, two leaders in sportswear for anglers and adventurers, do a great job in each of these areas. Take some long pants as well as shorts, and both long and short sleeve shirts. You need to be self-sufficient on the flats, so select shirts and pants with plenty of deep pockets.

A hat is also important. I dislike the long-bill type hats, particularly those with rims that cover the ears, but this is a personal thing more than anything else. They do work and eliminate the pain of sunburn. I like baseball hats instead, preferring to cover my ears and back of my neck with sun-screen. Take a light jacket or windbreaker, maybe even a light sweater or sweatshirt; it does get cool on the flats at times, and a rain jacket is a must as well. It can rain or downpour at any time, even in the "dry" season. For everyday footwear around the lodge or when not fishing a pair of light-weight sneakers, boat shoes or sandals are perfect.

RECOMMENDED GEAR FOR FISHING AND TRAVELING IN THE CARIBBEAN

- Fly rods (at least two)
- Fly reels (at least two)
- Flies
- Extra fly line
- Extra backing
- Leaders
- Tippet material
- Long-nose pliers/hook remover
- Polarized sunglasses (extra pair if available)
- Wading shoes
- Sunscreen (SPF 30 or better) and Lip Balm
- Swiss army knife or pocket knife
- Neoprene slippers or wading socks
- Camera and film
- Reading material
- Small flashlight and extra batteries
- Hat
- Clothing
- Rain gear
- Fanny pack
- Toilet kit: toothbrush, tooth paste, Insect repellent, anti-diarreal, first-aid kit, floss, mouth wash, shaver and shaving cream, after-shave, comb or brush, antiseptic, Band Aids, tweezers, antacid, AfterBite, required medicines, aspirin/non-aspirin substitute
- Boat shoes/sneakers/sandals
- Passport/airline tickets/camp vouchers

PLACES TO GO

It is not for me to question what the Almighty had in mind when He created what man would call the Caribbean. But I like to think the big guy likes to fly fish from time to time and simply wanted a near perfect environment for the pursuit of bonefish, tarpon and permit. Of course, I doubt that is the real reason. But the fact remains, the Caribbean basin represents the single most productive ecosystem on the planet for these fish, and those of us who reside on the west side of the Atlantic are fortunate to have it at our doorstep. No matter where you live in the Americas the Big Three are just a few hours away. But considering my home is in Maine, I appreciate this modern age. I have done my best over the years to take advantage.

TARPON

Seeing a giant tarpon slither through shallow water while on the prowl; the thrill of casting a fly across its path; experiencing the take; setting the hook and feeling the awesome power once the hook strikes home and witnessing its aerial mastery, all adequately describe what challenging this fish is truly like. Simply put, there is nothing quite like it. And once successfully done, nothing on the flats will ever be quite the same. The only thing you know is you want more.

Of course, the many attributes this fish has to offer the inshore angler are well known. They have been for decades, but there was a time not long ago when taking a tarpon on rod and reel was believed to be impossible. In his book, *Game Fish of North America*, the late great A.J. McClane quotes S.C. Clarke, who concluded in Charles Hallock's *Camp Life in Florida*, in 1876, "No man is strong enough to hold a large tarpon (sic) unless he is provided with a drag or buoy in the shape of an empty keg attached to a line, which may retard or even stop the fish after awhile."

I can fully appreciate his belief that a large tarpon is next to impossible for any mortal to subdue. On more than one occasion in the Florida Keys, Costa Rica and Belize when my spine felt it was about to snap twenty minutes into a successful hookup, this thought has crossed my mind as well. It is only out of sheer determination that I refuse to give up once the battle is well underway, despite the continuous pounding and those moments when my body and every bit of intelligence I possess questions the sanity in doing so.

When the contest is over, a silver beast stretching five or six

Tony Traad photo

A mass of swimming muscle, south Florida tarpon are among the biggest to be found in the Caribbean. A fish this size can take an hour to boat.

feet with a mouth the size of a bait pail and scales the size of license plates rises from the depths and shows its magnificence. It is then, when my heart skips a beat I realize I am just as dog-tired as my adversary. Yet, on each occasion other questions always remain. Was I just lucky? Will I be just as lucky another day? Or was it a measure of skill in conjunction with modern equipment which won the day? Most important of all, will I be able to do this when I am an old man? On this latter point, I have serious doubts.

With tarpon, these are questions for which I have yet to find the answer, but they are also reasons for spending much time in their pursuit while I still can. It is said some things are better not known. Maybe. I will be the first to admit I don't know everything there is to know about this fish, or catching them, but what I do know is tarpon and tarpon fishing are like a drug. They get under your skin and once addicted there is no turning back. While hooking and playing them, they are hooking and playing you. On the flats there is nothing quite like them, and while each one fought makes me feel older beyond my years it is a short-lived condition, and in reality, tarpon make me come alive like few other fish. Looking back on those I have had the pleasure of knowing, there is no doubt they have given me far more than they have received. And if I were to drop dead tomorrow my life as an angler would be complete because I have experienced the tarpon's wrath on a fly rod.

Within angling circles the tarpon is affectionately known as the "silver king." It holds the distinction of being one of the first, if not the first, marine specie to be designated a game fish,

Tying flies on a quiet evening at Rio Colorado Lodge. For those who tie their own flies, a small travel fly tying kit is handy.

and if there is any one fish more cherished among inshore anglers of south Florida it has not yet been created. In the Spanish-speaking countries of the Caribbean the tarpon is called "sabolo" but the scientific community knows it as *Magalops atlantica*. It is related to the herrings and the shads, and in appearance with its somewhat oblong, compressed body and flattened forehead looks much like its relatives.

Tarpon are dark bluish-silver to greenish-black along the back which quickly changes to bright iridescent silver or whitish along the sides. The entire fish from the gills back, except for the fins, is completely covered with heavy scales giving it the look of a knight of the Roundtable in silver mail. There are approximately 40 to 50 scales along the lateral line, and depending upon the size of the fish these scales vary in size from the size of a dime or quarter on small fish to larger than a silver dollar on the giants, those over 100 pounds. The glistening sheen of these fish is one of their most distinguishable features, particularly as they leap from the water and head for the heavens or begin to "bubble," the term used to describe the slowing down of a spent fish after a long fight and they approach the surface.

Another obvious body characteristic of the tarpon is its head. Everything about it is big. And tough! The mouth looks like a cannon-ball hole and is surrounded on both sides by scale-like rakes which help in the process of sucking in food. These rakes as I call them, along with the gill covers are sharp and extremely tough, one reason why shock-tippets are needed to subdue these fish, and why caution is a must and gloves should be worn when removing flies around the head area. The gill covers are so rigid that when a tarpon jumps and shakes its head, it is often possible to hear them rattle as they slap against the head. It is a magnetic yet unnerving sound, one not quickly forgotten, but a reminder of just how much power is on the end of the line and how much respect should be given when the fish comes boatside. The inside of the mouth is equally as tough and boney, making it a "no-hands zone," and setting a fly calls for sharp hooks and considerable pressure.

On many occasions after a battle I've thought if the tarpon had legs it would make a perfect boxer. Its lower jaw and large snout form ideal targets for a right jab, but considering the way they are built, and considering its strength and tenacity I doubt even a poke from Mike Tyson would have an effect. The lower jaw bone is large, extremely strong and projects up and in front of the upper part of the mouth. The two branches of the lower jaw are connected by a boney plate, called the "gular plate." I have seen guides slip a gaff through this area, and behind the lower jaw bone, to help hold and stabilize giant tarpon boatside. They claim the tactic causes no serious damage, but my desire is never to see any fish gaffed unless absolutely necessary. With tarpon, particularly those over 50 pounds, it generally is, but I prefer to see guides "lip-hold" them instead. The method is described under, "Hooking and Playing Tarpon," in this section.

The tail of a tarpon is also quite large and deeply forked, like all fast swimmers, and is extremely powerful. Putting it in boating terms it would be like putting a 100 horsepower outboard on a canoe! When it slaps the water just a few feet away, or the side of the boat, it soon becomes obvious just how big, and powerful. A word to the wise—stay clear of this potentially dangerous weapon whenever a tarpon is boatside. But even more incredible is how it helps these fish to be such master leapers. Scientists have measured vertical jumps as high as 10 feet, and horizontally more than 20 feet.

The tarpon's dorsal fin sits in the middle of the back. It, too, is relatively large but its most distinguishable feature is a long whip-like filament which on some large tarpon extends more than halfway to the tail. Although still unproven, to my knowledge, it is believed by some in the scientific community, and many anglers, that this appendage serves a purpose. It is mentioned here just as a point of interest, and has little value when a tarpon is on the rod.

Concave on its underside, much like a suction cup, when a tarpon leaps the filament swings and often sticks to one side of the fish and helps turn or secure the dorsal fin to the left or right. It is the dorsal fin which controls the direction of a tarpon's fall back to the water. In other words, if the dorsal is leaning to the right during the jump, the plunge back to the water will be to the right. The fall back to the water will be to the left if the dorsal fin is leaning to the left during the jump. Because the extended filament helps control and direct the dorsal fin, it also plays a role in which direction a leaping tarpon will fall back to the water.

In overall appearance, few will deny the tarpon is a most pleasing fish to gaze upon. Some would even call them beautiful. My opinion is not quite so generous. Although there is little doubt tarpon are a prime example of evolutionary craftsmanship, able to tolerate warm water, hunt extremely shallow water despite its size, and are among nature's most perfect eating machines on the flats. They lack aesthetic grace, form and coloring which normally defines outward beauty when describing wild creatures, but are so impressive, so unique it is difficult to take your eyes off them. To tell you the truth, I actually find tarpon rather plain looking, but I will be the first to admit I am overwhelmed each time I see one, when a battle is won and an example slides to the surface. It is one of anglings great sights.

It is the size of these fish, their length and awesome girth, and power which keeps me such a fan. Even small baby tarpon have a way of neutralizing an otherwise assertive and haughty spirit. In a nutshell, and without insulting myself further, no other fish makes me so insecure or feel so inadequate on the flats. Bonefish are testy and have a way of making you realize your mistakes; failure with permit is often unexplainable despite apparent perfection with rod and fly. Tarpon can be the same way, but they have other attributes which seem to work to some degree on all who seek them. They have an intimidation factor that overwhelms and unnerves the fisherman the minute one is spotted cruising shallow water. This is particularly true of fish over five feet which resemble a living, breathing torpedo below the water's surface.

Captain Tony Traad of Homestead, Florida is just one of many "trailer" guides who fish the Keys. Traad specializes in tarpon. Here he prepares to release a hefty tarpon near the Everglades.

They also seem to obliterate momentarily all forms of thinking when first sighted. No matter how good you are, or think you are, no matter how many success stories you have under your belt, seeing a giant tarpon is an awesome thing, one of the true wonders of nature, and along with forcing the angling mind to question the rationale of challenging such a beast with nothing but a fly rod, they can turn a genius into a babbling fool. I have caught dozens of tarpon over the years, and there are still times when I am held captive by their mere sight. It is a part of the game I hope I never lose. What bothers me most, however, is when I stand there on the deck frozen as the excitement and panic builds inside my gut, and I question my ability to do things right. I know what to do, and how to do it, but there are times when until I get over the initial shock of seeing my target my body refuses to respond.

But that is what tarpon and working the flats for this beast is all about. I realized early on I hunt these fish for the thrill of the hunt as much as casting a fly, and that achieving success is but an added bonus. Enticing tarpon to the fly is not consistently arduous, not like it is with permit or bonefish on some occasions. But due to their size and awesome presence there is no more ultimate challenge or bonus on the flats with a fly rod.

The tarpon is among the oldest of all fish. It was swimming earth's oceans thousands of years ago, and its appear-ance today is much the same. In essence, it comes to us basi-cally unchanged, and it would seem Mother Nature in her infinite wisdom was more happy with her initial creation and saw no reason to alter it through the ages as she has so many others. Had she known, however, that man would evolve into a sport fishing-maniac, and the tarpon would be one of the prime reasons for that insanity, I dare say the grand dame might have made a few minor changes. Then again, consider-ing the tarpon's size and tenacity, its natural-born ability to throw a fly, and desire to put the person on the end of a fly rod through hell if solidly hooked, maybe she saw no need for a change.

The tarpon is a fish that must truly breathe to survive. Not just by sucking in water through its gills and extracting oxy-gen in the process as many other fish do, but by using a lung-like internal swim bladder. This is why on quiet, windless flats it is sometimes possible for the trained ear to actually hear a tarpon before setting eyes on it. These fish must, on occasion, breech the surface to inhale air, much like a whale, and in the process their exhalation is sometimes obvious. In his book, *Tarpon Quest*, fellow Maine writer John Cole describes the event as a "sigh," ... "a sibilant sign, a mournful release quite unlike any other sound heard at sea, so laden with an immortal sadness." I have been present on Caribbean

waters as tarpon break the surface to fill or empty their oxygen load, and though I don't know if I would call it a "sigh," it is easy to see how it might be construed as such. Cole is right when he says, "that it stabs the conscience of your soul." It is something you don't soon forget, for not only is it a reminder tarpon are truly unique among game fish, the human reaction to this sound is similar to striking a match beneath a powder keg. It sets the adrenaline pumping through the veins at lightning speed and means the target you have been hunting for is close at hand.

Tarpon are unique in another way, too. They are among those special fish that can sustain themselves in a variety of water types. There is little doubt tarpon are more common in the more saline waters of the open flats, but they will frequent and are often found in brackish, turbid, even freshwater, although the latter must be calcium-rich and not susceptible to long periods of cold temperatures. Although it is not common, fishermen have caught tarpon as far inland as Lake Okeechobee in south Florida. They are considered common far into the mangrove backwaters of the Everglades, in the muddy, chocolate-colored rivers and lagoons of Costa Rica and Belize, and I know of several islands in the Caribbean with small ponds and lagoons with "freshwater" populations. Growing evidence suggests it is the tarpon's swim bladder that allows them to be so far ranging, but from an angling perspective it is really of little importance. What is important is tarpon are widely available, and offer some of the most challenging, and rewarding fly fishing opportunities the angling world has to offer.

A green-toed sloth, Rio Colorado Lodge, Costa Rica. This interesting specimen was found hanging outside the kitchen door. Wildlife and birds are plentiful.

DISTRIBUTION AND MIGRATION

Tarpon are residents in various parts of the world and are found in both tropical and subtropical waters. Although a rare occurrence, they have been spotted in the warm gulf stream as far north as Nova Scotia in the western Atlantic, and on the east side there is a developing sports fishery for the adventurous off the coast of Africa. Historically, south Florida and certain parts of the Caribbean are the center of the universe when it comes to taking this species on a fly.

But this does not mean to say tarpon are numerous everywhere within this geographic area. Tarpon are not, for example, abundant in the Bahamas. There are fishable populations in waters surrounding some of those enchanted and fish-rich isles, and some are caught, particularly around Andros Island. Their numbers can be surprising during spring migrations, but as a whole the Bahamas are not universally known as a tarpon hotspot.

Elsewhere in the Caribbean and parts of the western Atlantic, *Megalops atlantica* is well represented, either seasonally or as year-round residents. Most noteworthy as far as populations and angling opportunity go include places along the Yucatan Peninsula of Mexico and Belize, which probably offers the best visual angling opportunities for the species in the Caribbean. There are peak seasons, primarily April and May into early June but Belize has tarpon year-round. There is good fishing on mainland rivers starting in February right into July, and in November and December, and there is excellent ocean and flats action from August through October.

Belize is also home to tarpon in three sizes. This is somewhat unique considering many other areas with resident populations typically offer fish of one general size, with an occasional larger or smaller example contributing to the sports fishery. I assume this is due to the fact that along with its resident tarpon, waters here are also visited by a migratory population which contribute greatly to the "peak season" activity. Baby tarpon under 20-pounds are generally found along the mangroves, in the lagoons and creeks on the mainland; mediums up to 70-pounds are found both along the mainland and on the flats of offshore islands, and the giants, or *"grande tarpon"* which frequent inshore areas in season, are most common on the flats.

Both Honduras and Nicaragua have tarpon. I have seen them in both countries but have not caught them, and I have little doubt the potential for a world class sports fishery is high along both coasts, although at this time both remain undeveloped for the species. Possibly good are parts of the Honduran coast as it nears the Coco River, the border with neighboring Nicaragua, and especially the unexplored tropical rivers and coast of Nicaragua. They could very well be angling hotspots if fully explored and fishing camps were established. It will take some time before that happens due to

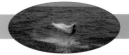

political and economic circumstances. And it would be a major undertaking to set up a lodge and network that world anglers would appreciate and feel comfortable with, but in the meantime I wouldn't mind being the angler doing the exploring.

Panama also has tarpon, and a few are known to have sneaked through the canal to the west coast, but here again, the fishery has yet to develop. Just up the coast, however, it is a different story.

For years Costa Rica, the "Rich Coast" as Columbus called it in 1502, has been internationally known as a tarpon-angling mecca. Destinations with names like Rio Colorado, Boca del Tortuguero and Boca del Parismina all have established fishing camps and lodges, and the number of anglers from around the world who flock there each year to work up a sweat fighting tarpon is impressive. Perhaps no other country in the Caribbean or in the immediate region, with the exception of the Florida Keys, is as popular a tarpon destination as this tiny nation that is about the size of West Virginia. And for good reason.

For one thing, tarpon are year-round residents. There are slow seasons, good seasons and peak seasons, with angling locales—either in the rivers or at their mouths, depending upon the season—but tarpon can be found and caught twelve months of the year. The tarpon are also known to be of medium and large size. Over the course of numerous trips to that delightful tropical hot spot and several dozen tarpon caught and brought to the boat, not one has been under 70 pounds. The largest was estimated at over 100 pounds, and I have been witness to even larger fish being taken.

The only drawback to this area, and it is only a matter of opinion, is the fishing is not the classic visual type that is so famous and popular in south Florida and Belize. The waters are typically muddy, carrying tons of silt from deep within the jungle to the sea, and tarpon are rarely seen. This is blind casting at its best, allowing the fly to sink and then waiting for a fish to locate the offering and strike. While it may not be the most demanding or challenging way to seek and lure tarpon to a fly, it is what works in these discolored waters. Because of the number of tarpon available, and the number of fish which can be caught each day, numerous hookups are not uncommon, my best day being eleven tarpon actually boated plus several lost. Costa Rica is prime testing area for the angler who has little experience battling large tarpon, and is the one place I would send a rookie looking to ply his luck.

As it is with bonefish, Venezuela is also home to tarpon. In fact it has been considered a hotspot tarpon destination for years, and although bonefish are more numerous and popular, the year-round tarpon opportunities leave little to be desired.

It should be noted, however, Venezuela is not known for big tarpon. Some giant and medium sized examples are seen and taken in the larger channels and lagoons and on some of the deeper flats, but the angler must really hunt for them and

The Seven Mile Bridge, connecting Pigeon Key and Little Duck Key, is an impressive achievement. It is a popular spot for tarpon as they pass from the Atlantic side of the Florida Keys to the Gulf.

be there at the right time of season. Once found they are not easy to approach or get on the fly. The majority of tarpon caught are baby-size, under twenty pounds. A good many are under 10 pounds. The primary reward for the lack of giant fish, and the main reason Venezuela is worth visiting for tarpon, is that bonefish can be caught on the same trip (as well as permit). There are lots of tarpon and high catch figures are possible, perhaps as many as fifty per day for the experienced rod. Even the novice can expect 10 to a dozen hookups if he or she is somewhat capable with a fly rod and uses some tact. There is also the pure joy of challenging and taking these fish on 7 or 8-weight tackle, rather than the heavier 10 and 12-weight kits normally used on larger tarpon.

On the northern edge of the Caribbean, Cuba offers some fine tarpon opportunities, particularly in the area of the Garden of the Queens, an amazing archipeligo about 90 miles off Cuba's south coast from the port town of Jucaro. The fish average under 20 pounds, although some larger fish frequent the area in the spring, but for the most part it is a resident, year-round population. Despite their small size catching them is not easy. The water is crystal clear and shallow in many areas providing good visibility and making tarpon extremely spooky of approaching boats, poorly placed flies, and flies that slap or hit the water too hard. Success demands precise casting into the mangroves, in some cases from distances of 30 to 40 feet, and always dropping the fly as gently as possible.

Unfortunately, Cuba and the fabulous bonefish and tarpon angling it affords is not open to American anglers. Hopefully,

someday it will be, and soon. At present, however, the "Queen of the Antilles" remains behind closed doors and the information provided here and on other pages is for anglers from Canada, Japan and other countries which allow residents access.

With the exception of Cuba, tarpon seem to be pretty much a mainland inhabitant within the Caribbean basin. Small populations are found in scattered locales from Jamaica and Haiti over to Puerto Rico and down through the Lesser Antilles, but not in such numbers they are worth traveling great distances to hunt down, particularly in light of the fact larger numbers, and more consistent and predictable angling opportunities are known elsewhere.

Tarpon are also represented on the North American continent, south Florida being the center of activity. In fact, the area from about Biscayne Bay in Miami on the east coast down through Islamorada, Marathon and Key West in the Keys, the Marquesas and the Dry Tortugas, and up the Gulf Coast to Homosassa Bay is the best known tarpon fishing grounds in the world. Starting in March, schools of giant tarpon begin to move onto the flats, and by May and June as more fish arrive on their annual migration, tarpon are everywhere. According to good friend Captain Tony Traad, who guides in Biscayne Bay, the Everglades and upper Keys, this is the peak time to hunt these waters, at no other time of year is there a better chance to take tarpon on a fly.

Tarpon are also known to frequent waters along the Louisiana and Texas coast, and some angling is done in both locales, but by no means can it compare to Florida or even other areas of the Caribbean.

One of the more interesting aspects of the tarpon is its migration. Although the species was one of the first to be designated a game fish, little is actually known about its migration route, or even where it goes after leaving inshore areas. During the cold months they seek warmer temperatures either in deep offshore locales or the Gulf Stream. It is interesting to note tarpon will move inshore even in January and February when water temperatures are cooperative and cold fronts don't keep them offshore. From a scientific standpoint a great deal more research needs to be done on the tarpon's migration, although anglers have long known when it's best to seek them out.

It should also be noted nearly all locations within the tarpon's range seem to have resident populations, even south Florida. They may not always be easy to locate, or entice to a fly. They are apt to move according to weather and water conditions, here one day and gone the next, but resident populations are present throughout the Caribbean nations and Florida. In general, permanent resident populations are largest and seem to be less migratory the further south and closer to the Equator you get, in Venezuela and Costa Rica, for example. The further north and away from the Equator, in Belize, the Yucatan and Florida, the smaller the resident numbers and the more dependent they are on annual migrations.

A tarpon rolls next to the boat after a long battle. The silver mail is most striking and their power and determination is often overwhelming. Few places in the Caribbean offer such productive tarpon action as Costa Rica, where it is possible for the novice to achieve success.

LIFE CYCLE AND SIZE

As it is with other members of this unique club, bonefish and permit, little is known concerning the tarpon's life cycle. The spawning season is presumed to take place between May and September, but the exact time during that period varies from one locale to the next.

It is believed tarpon spawn offshore and in south Florida during the spring. Tarpon larvae have been collected with their egg sacks still attached 100 miles in blue water in June. An adult female is apt to lay as many as 10 to 12-million eggs, and it is at this point the mystery begins. In the beginning these young tarpon-to-be are but a sliver of transparent skin with digestive tract, spinal structure and brain fully visible. Within six to eight weeks they reach a length of about one-and-a-half inches, and then, miraculously begin to shrink, one of a handful of fish to experience such a metamorphosis. Three to four months latter, at perhaps no more than an inch long, what emerges is a small juvenile tarpon, with fins, gill covers, eyes and other external parts all in place.

It is at this stage young tarpon head for shore where they seek shelter and protection in the myriad of backwaters, mangrove swamps and other hidden spots. There, in water ranging from salt to brackish to almost fresh, the young tarpon feed on plankton, eventually graduating to the larvae of crabs and mosquitoes and other aquatic insects, reaching a length of a foot or more in 10 months or less. A year or so latter, after stuffing themselves continuously, these young tarpon may reach miniature or baby size, generally 10 pounds or under. I like to chal-

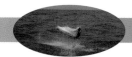

lenge these youngsters on light fly gear, in the 7 or 8-weight class, and find it one of the ultimate joys of inshore angling. Despite their relatively small size, baby tarpon pack a punch, are great leapers and battle with the same determination and tenacity as their older, heavier counterparts.

These young fish continue to grow fast, adding several pounds to their girth and perhaps a foot or more to their length each year until reaching full maturity. At that point growth continues, but at a slower rate. Currently, evidence suggests females typically reach larger sizes than males, it is believed a vast majority of the fish caught on rod and reel over 100 pounds are females. Also, females seem to reach sexual maturity between the ages of seven and 10, somewhere between 50 and 70 pounds, with males maturing at a younger age and smaller size.

It was once believed tarpon were short-lived, living only to 20 or 25 years of age, but scientists now believe these fish live to reach a ripe old age, perhaps as old as 45 or even 50 years. Whatever the case may be, tarpon live long enough to reach impressive size, and it is their weight and length which make them such an impressive and awesome prize. No other fish in skinny water has such a hypnotic hold on the angler, and while

Patrick Roberts, head guide at Oeisha's Resort, Sandy Point, Abaco, Bahamas prepares his boat for a day on the flats.

their power has a great deal to do with it, there is no question so does their size.

The demarcation weight of different classes seems to vary depending upon who you talk to. However, there seems to be a general acceptance that baby or immature tarpon are those under the 20-pound mark. Anything over that and up to about 50 pounds is considered small. Those between 50 and 100 pounds are considered large, with the giant category being anything over 100 pounds. Most of the fish caught on fly rod and reel fall within the two middle categories, from 20 to about 100 pounds.

Of the various weight classes, however, the giants are most impressive. I personally enjoy tarpon weighing in between 60 and 90 pounds. They seem to jump more, often higher, and they can burn a reel with the same blinding speed as their larger counterparts. On the other hand, I cannot deny my heart takes a pounding each time a fish over 100 pounds is hooked. Throughout their range fish of 120, 140 and 150 pounds are possible, and specimens well over 200 pounds have been boated on a rod and reel. My best is a 120 pound fish, taken off the mouth of the Rio Colorado in Costa Rica. I recall well the trouble I had and the punishment that fish put me through. I cannot imagine tackling something close to 100 pounds larger, although, like most tarpon fools I keep looking and can't wait to try, if only for a minute.

WATER TEMPERATURES AND SEASONS

Tarpon are sensitive to cold temperatures, and during sudden cold-snaps mortalities occur. Like bonefish, tarpon may test the flats when inshore temperatures are under 68 to 70 degrees F., but few will move inshore and remain until temperatures consistently reach 74 or 75 degrees. They tolerate water down to about 64 degrees and as high as 104 degrees, but their ideal temperature range seems to be 75 to 85 degrees.

Because of this temperature range, tarpon can be found somewhere pretty much any time of the year. This is true even in the Keys, although during the cold months they are seldom easy to find. From November through much of February, because they seem to be less migratory the majority of fish caught seem to be in the five to 50 pound class in many locales. This is certainly true in south Florida, Belize, Cuba and to a large degree Venezuela. An exception is Costa Rica, where it is possible to take 50-pound-plus tarpon virtually 12 months of the year.

In March, things start to heat up. Giant tarpon begin to appear around the outside islands in the Keys, and throughout the Caribbean basin tarpon are everywhere. In places like Belize, Costa Rica and Venezuela tarpon are moving into many of the rivers, and through June the opportunity to challenge these fish in moving water is good. I have been blessed in the sense that dozens of tarpon have illustrated their belligerence for me in stillwater over the years, on the flats and amongst the man-

groves, and each one is a fond memory. But to have a tarpon on the end of your line in moving water as an aid is an unparalleled experience. In a river like Costa Rica's Rio Colorado or the Belize River, a 50-pound tarpon feels twice its size, and in that environment playing these fish takes on a whole new dimension and can be as addictive as playing them on the flats.

April continues to offer excellent opportunities within the Caribbean basin, particularly for big fish. In Belize, large tarpon can be found on the flats, in the estuaries and mangrove bays. In the Garden of the Queens of Cuba, the resident population of small tarpon are joined by schools of migrating fish in the 50 to 80-pound class. In the fabulous Rio Chico region of Venezuela there are lots of tarpon at this time, and it is not unusual to strike or jump a dozen or more each trip out, but generally speaking they are not large. Most run under ten pounds, although it is possible to take an occasional 25 or 30-pounder. In Biscayne Bay and the Florida Keys, however, once water temperatures hit 74 or 75 degrees, just the opposite is true. It is in April when schools of spring giants arrive in reliable numbers, many exceeding 120 pounds. In May and June and into early July the best angling of the season is at hand. Tarpon are literally everywhere, on the flats, up and down the coastal beaches, in the mangroves and backwaters, in bays, canals and in the passes.

In Belize, at Turneffe Flats, perhaps the premier angling spot in the country, this is also a peak time for tarpon. Although tarpon are available year-round Turneffe's tarpon season runs from May into September, but June, July and August is considered the peak period. Examples near the 100 pound mark and slightly bigger are possible, and they are available in good numbers. This is also a prime time for a grand slam in Belize, considering both permit and bonefish are at hand.

The fall months, September into early December, can be hot or cold, depending upon were you go. This period can be dynamite in Costa Rica, and I have witnessed some of my best tarpon action off the mouth of the Rio Colorado in November. This is also a prime time in Venezuela, where increased water levels and fresh water flow into the Caribbean following the summer rainy season draws larger tarpon into the lagoons. In Belize tarpon are still available, but they are generally not as numerous and the action slows. Those tarpon also tend to be smaller in size than those caught in June, July and August. In Cuba there is a good number of small and baby tarpon and some in the 30 and 40-pound class are still on the prowl as well. In South Florida and the Keys, the fishing is less concentrated in September, but still reliable, particularly as tarpon begin to stuff themselves on the mullet run. This continues into October, especially on the east coast, but by November the larger fish have moved or are beginning to move into deep water and are more difficult to find with regularity. Some good action on smaller tarpon can still be found at the mouths of creeks, in some of the bays, rivers and canals, but even they can be spotty and irregular. January in the Keys can be tough, but in February and into March, find some warm water—in the 70 to 74-degree range—and you are apt to find fish.

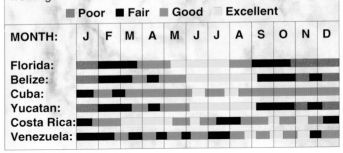

GENERAL TARPON TABLE

The following is a general time table for tarpon in different locales. While most areas offer tarpon year-round some periods are better than others. Keep in mind this is just a general scale. A great deal is based upon personal experience and times may vary depending upon local conditions. For more up-to-date conditions and information on timing interested fishermen should contact guides, lodges and booking agents working in those areas.

■ Poor   ■ Fair   ■ Good   □ Excellent

MONTH:	J	F	M	A	M	J	J	A	S	O	N	D
Florida:												
Belize:												
Cuba:												
Yucatan:												
Costa Rica:												
Venezuela:												

FOOD AND FLIES

The tarpon's mouth is huge, and seems capable of inhaling anything from the size of a golf ball to a basketball. There seems to be little doubt that few food stuffs go unnoticed. When opportunity knocks tarpon suck down what is available. Like most game fish, they appear to have certain preferences, amongst the favorite tidbits are mullet, crabs, shrimp, pinfish, scaled sardines, various marine worms, needlefish and squid, and a great many others, depending upon the area.

Traditionally, however, as with many saltwater flies, tarpon fly design has been rather basic, and for the most part it holds true even today. There seems to be a trend of late, however, particularly in the Keys, of tying and utilizing more imitative-type designs to take advantage of seasonal availability of certain foods. In their most informative book, *Backcountry Fly Fishing*, Doug Swisher and Carl Richards address this new avenue of thought, and based upon my personal experience with some rather fussy tarpon, it has merit. It only makes sense if the angler can provide a fly that resembles the natural food tarpon are interested in, the end result will be greater success.

The problem is, except for the mullet run in early fall and the Palolo worm hatch in the spring, much remains to be discovered, documented and made available for the angling public about the major foods in the Keys, when they are most readily available, and particularly concerning the fly designs which best imitate them. At present not a great many imitative tarpon flies exist on the commercial market and unless you tie your own they are difficult to come by. In several tying books, such as *Saltwater Fly Patterns* by Lefty Kreh, *Flies for Saltwater* by Dick Stewart and Farrow Allen and *Saltwater Flies: Over 700 of the Best* by Deke Meyer, some interesting designs which take the traditional tarpon streamer design a step further are now listed—the Stearn's Pinfish, Phil's Dahlberg Shrimp and Phil's Terminator

Shrimp being just three. What I would classify as "imitative" designs are far outnumbered by their "non-imitative" counterparts. And in general the vast majority of tarpon in Florida and the Caribbean continue to be taken below the surface on streamer patterns that have been around for years.

Putting together a productive assortment of tarpon flies is not that difficult. For the novice enthusiast unfamiliar with a given area, however, or even the experienced hunter fishing an area for the first time, it always helps to know what works, or what should work. I have been traveling and casting flies in tarpon water for years and I still make a habit of asking routine questions: "What are they hitting?" "Any particular color or colors?" "What size?" During the planning stage of any trip, whether with a guide, by direct contact with a tarpon camp or through representatives or booking agents, it is always a good idea to inquire what offerings should be taken. It is also helpful to keep in mind many tarpon camps and their booking agents will supply a recommended list of tackle and flies upon request, along with information on the establishment and other helpful data.

There are, however, some general guidelines the tarpon angler should keep in mind. For example, many of the most popular designs and best known tarpon flies come in a rainbow of color combinations, some gaudy and bright, some in natural tones. They come in a variety of sizes, just like streamers used for other game fish. An arsenal in light and dark dressings should be on hand. Because bottom conditions along with water clarity differs greatly from one area to the next, even from day to day. Dark flies seem to have better visibility over a light bottom and in clear water, while light or bright flies show up better over a dark bottom and in discolored surroundings. The angler wants to be prepared and ready to adapt to varying conditions.

Personally, I prefer dark flies, those in all black and all brown, and these shades incorporated with red, yellow or orange. Offerings with these color combinations seem to work just about everywhere, from the Florida Keys to Venezuela, Costa Rica to Cuba. In general, black is a good shade for these fish, as are various shades of brown, from dark hues to light. Based upon personal experience, however, I also consider other color combinations just as important. Anything with red/white, orange/yellow, red/orange and red/yellow, for example is apt to produce a strike wherever tarpon are found. Purple/orange and purple/red combinations are good, too, as are flies carrying some peacock herl, Krystal Flash or Flashabou. Offerings constructed in the natural tones can be good, too, and don't over-

Despite its poverty Cuba is a beautiful country. It is understandable why it is called the "Queen of the Antilles". Some towns date back to the 1600s, and the architecture is most interesting.

look crab and shrimp patterns. Tarpon love them and at times they produce results when all else to fails.

What draws attention and makes tarpon strike is never certain. Independent guides and guides working at specific camps generally have a darn good idea, so be sure to inquire, but more than one guide has been made a fool of, so take what is recommended plus the biggest selection you can afford or put together in an array of color combinations. It may be a bit costly or time consuming, and you may not use them all each day out, or even on a single trip. But then again, I have experienced times when just about every fly in my arsenal, and that means 30 or 40 different color combinations, was tried unsuccessfully before tying one on that finally worked. The truth is, you just never know, so go prepared .

Fly size is also important. In fact, there have been times when I was firmly convinced fly size had more to do with success than color. On my maiden trip to Cuba someone recommended tarpon flies in size 1/0 to 3/0. When I got there, however, I found the water to be crystal clear and quite shallow in many areas with the tarpon averaging under 20 pounds and in order to hook them, dropping flies close or beneath the mangroves was called for. No matter how hard

South Florida and the Florida Keys, from Biscayne Bay to the Marquseas, offers some of the finest fly fishing opportunities for bonefish, permit and tarpon in the world. The area is home to some of the angling world's finest guides and equipment, and they all speak English!

I tried the large flies slapped the water too hard, spooking more than I hooked. I eventually started using the same color combinations but on size 1 and size 2 hooks and my strike ratio and the number of fish hooked and released increased dramatically.

Tarpon come in different sizes so flies should be available in different sizes as well. Generally speaking, considering the size of the fish most tarpon flies are relatively small and sleek. Most run from about two inches to four inches in length. For truly

giant tarpon in deep water, off Florida's west coast and off the mouth of some jungle rivers, like the Rio Colorado in Costa Rica, or when tarpon appear to be just hanging below the surface in shallow water and not moving, a larger offering from perhaps five to as much as seven inches might be needed. When it comes to hook sizes, however, for tarpon over 50 or 60 pounds sizes 3/0 to 5/0 should be considered. For tarpon between 20 and 50 pounds sizes 1/0 and 2/0 work well; for tarpon around 10 or 15 pounds sizes 1 and 2, and for smaller tarpon hooks down to size 4 are more than adequate.

Although there is no demarcation line governing hook size to fish size, a good general rule is the smaller the fish, the smaller the fly, and vice versa. Other factors must also be considered, however. The bigger the fly the more difficult it is to cast, particularly in the wind, so if you have trouble working 40 to 50 feet of fly line when the breeze is up, drop down a size or two, even if big fish are in the area. If working extremely skinny water, the surface is mirror calm or fish appear spooky, a smaller sized fly might also be to your advantage. Keep in mind, too, the larger the hook the more difficult it is to drive into the tarpon's bony mouth. If you are not accustomed to setting large hooks, go with something a size or two smaller.

Overall, for the size tarpon I prefer to catch, and for tarpon from 40 to 80 pounds, hook sizes 1/0 and 2/0 are generally more than sufficient. I know many guides and experienced tarpon enthusiasts who rarely use anything larger. An exception is when larger tarpon, those in excess of 90 pounds, are working the area. In the vast majority of cases, however, sizes 1/0 and 2/0 have all the holding strength you need. They are also easier to cast, easier to set, and in those shallow, calm water situations are less apt to slap the water on the final cast.

Tarpon flies are available in two basic streamer designs, and which to use is determined by the type of water being fished. Perhaps the oldest and best known is the Keys-style. These are sleek, sparsely tied creations with the wing attached just above the bend in the hook, and which carry a collar in front of the wing laid back towards the tail. The shank can be totally exposed, but the majority are built to a tapered head with thread. The head is then either covered with lacquer or epoxy, or painted before being lacquered.

Keys-style tarpon flies of old were quite long, some in the five and six-inch range. The wing was attached near the bend to prevent the wing from fouling or wrapping around the hook during the cast. Modern counterparts are generally much shorter, from two to four inches, but the basic design remains the same. The wings are constructed of various materials including neck and saddle hackles and marabou which on some specific patterns are incorporated with a few strands of bucktail, Krystal Flash or Flashabou. Rabbit fur, calftail, grizzly hackle and FisHair are other materials used in the wings. Of these materials saddle and neck hackles are most popular, particularly the latter since they seem to flare better and are stiffer, and less apt to foul around the hook. The Keys-style fly is extremely popular and is used just about everywhere tarpon are found, particularly on the flats and other clear, shallow water situations where fish can be seen, or sight casting is the norm.

Another type of tarpon fly is the Whistler, first conceived by west coast fly fisherman and writer Dan Blanton. Unless fishing deep, your fly should not sink too quickly since it is a rare occasion when tarpon will descend to accept it. Ideally, the fly should be fished at the same level as the fish, or slightly higher where it can be easily seen. There are times, however, when tarpon are deep, or deeper than when on the flats, and getting down is necessary.

The Whistler design carries a heavy wing, a thick palmered collar or body, and is generally weighted with lead wire tied in front of the wing and large bead eyes. This is a deep water offering, but it has also become a standard in discolored or muddy water like the Rio Colorado in Costa Rica where I first used them. The large bead eyes, bulky wing and palmered head seems to push water and vibrate beneath the surface making it easier for tarpon to locate them and greatly increasing its effectiveness. Like the Keys-style flies, the Whistler can be tied in a myriad of colors and color combinations, and is a must when fishing tarpon in deep water or when visibility is greatly reduced. This design can also be tied unweighted, this can be a major advantage even in muddy or discolored shallow situations.

Other streamer designs are used to catch tarpon, too. A prime example is the Deceiver, perhaps the most popular fly used in saltwater. The Deceiver can be tied to swim deep, at medium depths or just below the surface. This fly is tied in various sizes and with the wing hackles flared inward to obtain a sleek appearing look or outward for maximum tail action. It can also be tied in a multitude of color combinations using a variety of materials. Although not specifically designed for tarpon, the Deceiver is a universal offering that works extremely well on tarpon of all sizes and in just about any water situation.

Don't forget all hooks must be sharp, but this is particularly true for tarpon. The mouth is extremely tough, and to penetrate that toughness make it a rule to check your hooks and sharpen them before they are attached to the leader. You will be glad you did. Either the triangular method, shaping the two sides into a "V" with a top giving you three supporting edges, or the diamond method can be used, but the important thing is to make sure those hooks are sharp before going to work.

Unless the angler desires to imitate the predominant baitfish that tarpon are feeding on, or that are in the particular local at a given time, putting together a good selection of flies is not that difficult and can be as easy as making a simple inquiry before leaving home.

In review, unless fishing deep or discolored water the Keys-style flies are the ones to go with. Have some available in different sizes, from 4, 1 and 2 for baby and small tarpon to 3/0 and 5/0 for giants, but go heavy on the 1/0 and 2/0 for those in the 40 to 80-pound class. Carry flies in an array of colors and color combinations, and take plenty. If fishing areas where water conditions are known to offer poor visibility, or if you think tarpon will be deep go armed with some Whistlers. And just for added measure, look into the Deceiver patterns as well. I make it a general rule to carry all three, and feel confident in being able to handle just about any situation that might arise.

Finally, it should be pointed out tarpon are one of those rare inshore breeds which under the right conditions find poppers attractive and will nail offerings on the surface. This is especially true with baby and small tarpon under 20 pounds when they are holed up in mangroves, or when fish are in the back coves, canals or other similar locales. This is also true of larger tarpon as well. Casting surface offerings to tarpon is much like casting to largemouth and smallmouth bass. It is not necessarily easy, in fact, it can be downright demanding even for experienced casters. But to have one of these gamesters rise and suck in a popper is one of the great joys the species offers. Have some poppers on hand whenever heading for tarpon country.

Following is a list of popular tarpon flies. Many are available at local tackle and fly shops and at some lodges throughout south Florida and the Caribbean where tarpon are a prime target. Many are also available from various fly shops and retailers offering mail order services. A partial listing will be found following "Part 3" of this book. For those interested in tying their own flies, the books mentioned earlier in this section authored by Deke Meyer, Dick Stewart and Farrow Allen and Lefty Kreh are good sources. Keep in mind this list is not all-inclusive, and many other patterns are available.

TARPON FLIES

Apte Tarpon Fly
Apte Too*
Black Death*
Baby Tarpon Fly*
Blanton's Finger Mullet
Brown/Orange Grizzly
  Bunny
Bleeding Tarpon Fly
Cockroach*
Casa Mar Special*
Cactus Baby Tarpon Fly*
Chris' Green/White Bunny
  Needlefish Kraft Fur
  Shrimp
Chinese Claw
Deceiver
Deepwater Tarpon Fly*
Deepwater Whistler*
D.L.'s Barred Tarpon Fly
Emery Orange
Estaz Collar Tarpon Fly
Gold-Brown Marabou
Tarpon Fly
Homosassa Deceiver
Homosassa Special
Huff Backcountry Fly

Huff's Ballyhoo Tarpon Fly
Huff's White Lightning
Jack's Favorite Black
Chugger
Jim Buck Squid*
Johnny's Needlefish
Keys Tarpon Streamer
Lenny's Chartreuse
Cockroach
Moore's Yellow and
Orange   Grizzly
Olch's Tarpon Glo*
Palolo Worm
Pate's Little Brown
Rhodes Tarpon Fly
Red and White Tarpon Fly
Stearn's Pinfish
Sea Bunny*
Seafoam Popper*
Smiley Needlefish*
Squirrel Tail
Steve Huff's Tarpon Fly
Tarpon Finger Mullet
Tarpon Grizzly*
Whistler*

✱Some patterns are available in a wide variety of color combinations or are the same basic fly tied with different materials, such as the Yellow/Green Deceiver and Red/White Deceiver, or the Black Whistler and Red/White Whistler, the Cactus Purple/Black Baby Tarpon Fly and Cactus Chenille Baby Tarpon or and the Black Tarpon Bunny and Red/Orange Tarpon Bunny, among others. They are listed collectively as Deceiver, Whistler, Cactus Baby Tarpon Fly and Tarpon Bunnys. These and other fly patterns which fall within the criteria are followed by an asterisk.

LOCATING AND SPOTTING TARPON

Unlike fishing for bonefish and permit, which is often a one-on-one endeavor, perhaps with a guide nearby, most tarpon fishing is conducted from a boat with a guide pointing out fish and instructing from just a few feet away. The job of a guide is not necessarily to teach, but many do, either purposely or as part of their demeanor. Their advice and expertise, even from those who are less instructive and more businesslike, no matter in what tone it may come is priceless. The best way to learn not only how to spot and recognize tarpon and other gamesters on the flats, but also how to approach and cast to them as well as the proper retrieve in different circumstances is to heed their advice. What the average angler would learn and

discover solo in several months, perhaps years, can be forever locked in the memory in just a few days with a guide. For the serious tarpon fan, it will be the best money ever invested.

Still, there are certain things that can be addressed here which might prove helpful. For example, of the three adversaries discussed in these pages—bonefish, tarpon and permit— tarpon are generally the easiest to spot in skinny water. This is due to their size and their coloration and the fact they are generally school fish.

The average sized tarpon caught on fly rod and reel runs 40 to perhaps 80 pounds, and that is a big object to see. When on the flats in water offering good clarity the dark blue or greenish-black along the tarpon's back can stand out like a sore thumb. Even smaller tarpon can be easy to detect because of this attribute. Regardless of size, they appear like dark, ghostly forms traveling in formation below the surface, and it is this darkened movement which is often first observed. If the water is clear, and depending on its depth, the cloud cover and the angle at which the fish are seen, the tarpon's silver armor may also reflect the sun, making it appear brighter than the bottom and the water around it. It reflects flashes like a mirror in the sun, but somewhat softer and more subdued.

In some situations, tarpon appear to be nothing more than an eerie shadow, a blur sliding through the water, and can be more difficult to spot. However, considering their size, dark top, bright sides, plus the fact there is usually more than one fish, these fish definitely stand out from their surroundings and are not as difficult to spot as bones and permit. The advantage of being above the water is that it greatly increases your visibility.

Tarpon sun themselves from time to time, and travel or roll with upper fins exposed. Always be on the lookout for dorsal fins and tails above the surface line. In low-light conditions early or late in the day, or when the sun is hidden by cloud cover, look for anything unusual such as nervous, ripply water or water being pushed. Bubbles rising to the surface are often an indication tarpon are at hand, and always be on the lookout for fish rolling or rising and gulping in air. During this process tarpon often extend much of their head above the surface.

In many situations intuition plays a role in catching tarpon, particularly in low-light conditions when the fish cannot be seen. If you think you see something that might be a fish, cast to it. It just might be a tarpon.

The art of spotting tarpon, as well as bonefish and permit, boils down to developing an observant eye, learning to recognize telltale signs and trusting your intuition. Again, in a great many cases a guide will be there working with you, and undoubtedly will spot tarpon before you, so memorize the indicators they point out.

Locating tarpon is not that difficult in a good many cases. This is generally the task of guides, and whether fishing in the Keys and hiring an independent or fishing out of a lodge in Belize or Costa Rica, these guys know where to find action according to the season. For the angler who likes to go it alone, however, when the season is in full swing tarpon are apt to be

found just about anywhere. That includes out on the flats, along the beaches, in canals, in ponds and rivers. Tarpon are often found in some of the most unlikely, out-of-the-way places imaginable.

When not on the flats and hunting food these fish like structure and certain places have a higher chance of holding fish than others. They like shaded areas and spots where shaded water meets the sun, so overhanging mangroves and overhanging banks are a must for investigation. So are areas around logs, rock piles and the edges of sandbars, particularly where shallow water meets deep water. Oyster beds should always be looked over with great care and are worth a few casts, as are the mouth of creeks where fast water meets a slower current or clean water mixes with dirty. Remember, tarpon breathe air so if you locate a spring hole give it careful scrutiny. Open areas, piers, docks, sea walls, beneath bridges and around bridge pilings and jetties all hold tarpon at some time and should not be overlooked.

Finally, study charts and get to know the tides. Tides are the key factor governing where tarpon will be at certain times and how actively they are feeding. This is also true of bonefish and permit and all inshore species.

CASTING AND RETRIEVING

One of the great thrills of fishing tarpon water is witnessing a pod of fish as they navigate the flats, especially as they maneuver into casting range. Few inshore species can accelerate the heart rate or obliterate all rational thinking quicker. For many it can be a most humbling experience, even frightening for few fish on the flats or in skinny water are as big and powerful.

I consider myself fairly adept at handling a fly rod, both in terms of distance and accuracy, yet tarpon have a way of always making me question my ability. Whatever it is I feel at the time, often collides with my deep desire to do things right and the knowledge that I want that fish so much. Often tarpon offer only one shot at success, perhaps two if the gods are with you, and to miss that opportunity can be utterly frustrating.

The key to casting is to relax, remember what you are doing, stay cool, be prepared for anything and never overestimate your abilities. Most guides will inquire of your casting ability before fish are even spotted. Some may even ask you to demonstrate— from different angles and into the wind—simply to determine your capabilities and range. Don't take it personally. The idea is to get you onto a fish, and knowing what you can do beforehand is a strategic advantage and key to your success. Even guides who don't ask would rather be told by you that a fish is out of range or at a difficult angle rather than have you make a mistake. Most guides will also check your drag. Initially it should be set rather light, enough to keep the line from backlashing yet free enough so line can easily be taken out when the strike comes. It can be reset once the hook is solidly in place.

You should be able to cast a tight loop between 40 and 60 feet with a degree of speed and accuracy. That means in traditional overhand fashion, but if possible it is a major advantage to achieve this distance using a sidearm cast as well. There are times when keeping the rod and line, and presenting the fly, low to the water is required to reduce glare, present a more delicate fly or to get an offering into some tight locales, and casting sidearm will allow you to reach those goals. If you have trouble casting, especially making quick, accurate deliveries and maintaining tight loops with heavy, bulky flies, it is highly recommended you practice or take a class before heading south. Viewing instructive videos, such as those available from Scientific Anglers will also help. There are also excellent sections on casting in *Fly Fishing Strategy* by Doug Swisher and Carl Richards.

The Caribbean is home to many birds, animals and other interesting critters. Iguanas are frequently seen sunning in warm, out-of-the-way places.

Brian O'Keefe photo

Equally as important, however, is being prepared to make a quick presentation of the fly. Sometimes tarpon will be discovered holding, other times moving extremely slow, appearing not to be moving at all, but usually tarpon are on the move when first spotted. This means two things—you will be casting to a moving target, not always the easiest endeavor, and it is necessary to get the fly to the fish quickly and in a position where it will be seen. The tarpon's eyes are on the side of its head, and its large snout partially blocks frontal vision. This means the ideal "strike zone" is within just a few feet to the side of the tarpons head. It is amazing how willing such a large fish is to turn and suck in a three-inch streamer, and how adept they are at it. The chances of hooking the fish also increase if it strikes from the side. Casting in front of the fish is an option, certainly better than casting too far back, behind or directly on top of the target. This is the quickest way to spook any fish, tarpon included.

The fly should land to the side of the head or in front of the tarpon. The fly should have time to sink to the same level as the fish. It should be worked across the tarpon's path or better yet in the same direction, so the two collide. Rarely are you successful casting to a fish swimming away and working your fly directly towards the tarpon. In the cat-and-mouse game of eat-or-be-eaten, nature doesn't work this way. Bait is always heading away from predators or unexpectedly swimming across their course.

How far in front of the fish your fly should be placed depends upon several factors—the fly's sink rate, water depth, how deep your target is and particularly how fast it is moving. It may be as few as two or three feet away, always a risky proposition, or perhaps 10 or 20 feet. The angler, with the help of the guide must gauge the situation, and deliver the fly accordingly. The closer you cast to the fish, the greater your chances of spooking it. Learn to read the situation and drop the fly well in front of the fish giving it time to sink to the proper level and allowing enough time to work it into proper position.

Each situation is different. Tarpon are seen in singles, pairs or in schools, and at times they are even viewed swimming on a circular course, one fish in back of the other swimming in a circle is called a "daisy chain." It is always a no-no to cast into a school of fish. Instead, cast ahead of the lead fish or pick out a larger fish if it is in the right position and make it your target. This minimizes the threat of spooking the others in the group and, in the event the lead fish or chosen target refuses what you have to offer, you still have a chance at one of its followers. When casting to fish in a daisy chain, the same rule applies. Never cast into the center of the circle. Toss to the outside and work it as close to the circle as possible and in the same direction the fish are traveling.

The key is to false-cast as little as possible, it is simply a waste of time. It also reduces the chance of fly line and fly spooking the target. Keeping that in mind, whatever length of line you expect to cast, whether it be 40 feet or 80 feet, it should be stripped from the reel, coiled on the deck and ready to shoot. Fifteen to 20 feet of line (more if you can handle it) should extend past the rod tip and loop back to your free hand. Keep the rod tip pointed slightly upwards or off to the side to keep the line free and off the water. When ready to cast roll the rod forward taking the excess line beyond the tip and helping load the rod, then shoot the remaining excess line off the deck on the back and/or forward cast.

One common problem when shooting line this way is the fly line becomes tangled as it lifts off the deck, and few things in casting are as frustrating as having line snarl when the desire is to get to a fish in a hurry. This problem can be eliminated. Before fish are spotted, strip off the desired length of line and make a cast, then retrieve the line and coil it on the deck. When ready to cast a second time for real, this allows line to lift off the deck from top to bottom, rather than from bottom to top.

Once the fly hits the water lower the rod tip, strip in any excess trying all the while to keep a watchful eye on the fly and your target. Ideally the offering should hit the water as close to the target as possible without spooking it, or cross its path quickly but at the proper level, when this happens the response is often immediate. If not, the tarpon may follow the fly before striking, but in any event be prepared to make any necessary adjustments. If it looks like the target is going to cross the point of intersection early, speed up the retrieve to cover ground. If it appears the fly will get there too soon, slow down the retrieve. The important thing is that both reach the same point at the same time and at the same depth. In general, the best tarpon retrieve is slow, with short, steady pulls that draw the fly from six to 20 inches, and allow it to pulsate through the water. Quick flicks of the wrist help give the fly a more lifelike action.

HOOKING AND PLAYING TARPON

When a tarpon trails a fly or is ready to strike most novice enthusiasts commit their greatest sins. Among other things they stop the retrieve, which nearly always makes the fish loose interest, or they speed up the retrieve not realizing tarpon seldom travel too far or too fast in pursuit of forage; only if the fish starts to veer off might a faster retrieve revive its interest, as if the "bait" is trying to escape, or they strike or try to set the hook prematurely, generally lifting the rod in the process.

It is difficult with so much excitement building inside you, but sustaining the same speed of retrieve until the fly has been accepted is a must, tarpon are somewhat lazy when it comes to chasing their meals and prefer to inhale prey that simply swims along. So keep your rod level with the water until the hook has been firmly set.

When to strike depends a great deal upon what angle the tarpon is about to attack the fly. If coming straight on from behind, maintain your steady retrieve, when the fly is inhaled the fish will generally turn left or right, and you will feel resistance. At this point immediately stop stripping. This allows the fly to be swallowed deeper and reduces the chance of pulling the fly out of the tarpon's mouth. Wait two or three seconds, and then while the fish is still in its turn or swimming away, keeping the rod low, strike hard two or three times by pulling straight back on the line with your free hand and sweeping the rod to the right or left in the opposite direction the tarpon is swimming. Doing so gives the hook maximum angle for penetration. If the tarpon strikes from the side, the better of the two scenarios, it will generally roll during the strike. The fly is deep inside the tarpon's mouth at this point, and as it moves away during its roll the fly generally hooks itself. Keeping the rod tip low the angler can definitely feel this when it happens, and should immediately draw back hard on the line to set the hook.

Once the hook is set all hell will break loose! The most important thing to do at this point is make sure line is free and clear of feet and any other objects. There is no time to waste. The tarpon's response is a quick one, almost instantaneous, so the angler must respond accordingly, not doing so can result in loss of the fish and is also dangerous. When making sure the line is clear raise the rod tip to about 45-degrees and position the reel seat under your forearm to prevent line from wrapping around the butt, form an open fist with your free hand to help keep the line straight and tangle-free as it is being stripped out and to assist it to the stripping guide. Many prefer to form an O-ring with their thumb and index finger. Both work. But the important thing is to get that excess line off the deck without it getting tangled.

The battle is now on! Tarpon typically make powerful, lightning-speed runs, often coupled with a series of leaps. About the only thing the angler can do for the next few minutes is hold on. There is no way to stop these fish when they make uncontrolled

runs, so don't try. As I do with Atlantic salmon, steelhead, bonefish, permit and other powerful adversaries I generally keep my rod level with the water and the tip pointed directly at the fish during these long initial runs. Many experts preach raising the rod, but keeping it low and pointing it at the fish in the beginning when the fish is fresh, reduces friction within the drag system and takes a good degree of pressure off the leader and connecting knots as more and more line is stripped out. When the fish slows, or between runs, I pump upwards and maintain a high rod tip, putting pressure on the fish by increasing drag or sliding one hand up the rod between the handle and stripping guide, reeling in excess line only as I lower the rod.

Two things must be kept in mind when playing big game fish, particularly tarpon. The first is to always keep the fish off balance. Once some line has been retrieved and the fish has slowed as it maneuvers one way, apply pressure in the opposite direction. This is the quickest way to subdue and tire a big fish while maintaining control.

And second, don't forget tarpon are great jumpers, and when they do it is necessary to establish "controlled slack." This reduces pressure on line, leader and knots and helps eliminate the chance aerial tarpon will not roll on the line and break free. This has traditionally been done by "bowing" the rod, or throwing excess line directly towards the fish as it clears the water,

hence the familiar phrase "bow to the king!" This technique works, and many guides will claim when a fish is lost during a jump it is because "you didn't give him enough free line," or "didn't bow the rod enough." The problem is that once the fish hits the water again the line may be slack, and during the rapid and frenzied process of retrieving it the fly may come free. It is at this point, not just during the actual jump, when a good many tarpon are lost.

Instead, it is often best to merely dip the rod tip when a tarpon takes to the air. It accomplishes the same basic thing. It allows the line to hang free, plus when the fish hits the water again the rod can immediately be lifted and excess line comes tight much sooner. It may not sound as romantic as "bowing to the King" but based upon personal experience it works just as well.

Playing tarpon can be difficult, physically-demanding work. Depending upon angler skill and experience a tarpon weighing 70 or 80 pounds can take 15 to 20 minutes or longer to subdue. A fish over 100 pounds can take the better part of an hour, and every minute is a test of endurance and determination among both parties, even if the angler uses all the right tricks and tries to bring the fish in quickly. Maybe. Maybe not!

You have made all the right moves, keeping the fish off balance, applying pressure when pressure was called for, "bowing"

The capable hands of Captain Bill Curtis of Miami, Florida illustrating the proper way to hold a fly rod and line when fishing for tarpon.

Tarpon are magnificent leapers, typically clearing the water a half dozen times or more during the battle. When they take to the air the angler must "bow" his rod.

or dipping the rod when needed and the battle is about to come to a close. The tarpon rises to the surface and "bubbles," or gasps in air. Exhausted, it rolls on its side displaying its silver mail and comes boatside as gently as a newborn babe. Your day is won. It is an exciting encounter for the great beast pants like a marathoner after a great race and to set eyes on such a magnificent creature brings out the most human of emotions. Treat it with care, revive and release it quickly, for it has earned that respect.

Or just the opposite may be true. Just when you are convinced you are the better gladiator, generally when the boat, the angler or guide is first spotted, and often within feet of the boat, the tarpon suddenly finds a new lease on life and either makes another mad dash or again takes to the air. Although this final surge may be short-lived, it is sudden, often powerful and takes the angler completely by surprise. It is then when a good number of tarpon are lost, for the angler is off guard. The possibility of a second wind can be reduced greatly by constantly applying reverse pressure on the fish during the battle and as the battle comes to an end. As the fish nears the boat or seems to tire but makes a dash to the right, lower the rod tip and apply pressure left, and keep doing it. Always apply pressure in the opposite direction until the fish is boatside.

But when a tarpon does get a second wind, simply allow the fish to run and get back into your fighting mode, applying reverse pressure as soon as possible. The fish is already tired, and some added pressure in the right spots will generally cut the new struggle for freedom short. Just to play it safe, maintain pressure until the fish is firmly under the guide's control. Many will instruct you to do so, letting you know when to provide slack. Take heed and follow his instructions. Also, take care when the fish is boatside and expect the unexpected. Tarpon can always roll or slap their tail even when they appear to be rather docile, and they can cause bodily damage.

Before heading out, take a few minutes to discuss the dos and don'ts with your guide, particularly if something is unclear. What is the right retrieve? How best to strike a fish? What to do once a fish has been struck? What is the best way to play a tarpon? Make sure the guide checks your drag and is aware of your casting limitations and experience.

EQUIPMENT

Rods

For fishing small and medium tarpon in the back country, an 8-1/2 to 9-foot rod designed for size 7, 8 or 9 is more than sufficient. These rods are light, easy to use, make it easier for most casters to throw tighter loops, and are better in many cases than longer counterparts at fighting and landing fish. My personal favorite is 8-1/2-feet for size 8 line. For small baby tarpon, those of just a few pounds, a 7-1/2 to 8-footer designed for size 6 line will do quite nicely. Whenever hunting larger fish, however, say tarpon over 70 pounds, rods designed to handle size 10 to 12 lines are the norm. I still like an 8-1/2-footer even with the heavier lines, I find them easier to cast and much better at taming heavy tarpon than the longer, and generally more giving and unwieldy, 9 and 9-1/2-footers.

In the end, however, rod selection boils down to what you like, what feels comfortable and what you can handle, particularly when hunting medium and large tarpon. It makes no sense to try casting with a 9-foot rod designed for a 12-weight line if you cannot cast it properly. Instead, go with a 9-footer, or even 8-1/2-footer designed for size 10 or 11 line. It will do just about everything the larger rod will, and be easier to use.

If you plan to spend a great deal of time and effort in tarpon country fishing different habitat you can't get away with just one rod. You need at least a couple, perhaps one for size 7, 8 or 9 line, and another for size 10, 11 or 12 line. It is always a good idea to travel with more than one rod anyway. To do otherwise would be like driving cross country with no spare tire. Rods have a nasty habit of getting lost in transit, dropped overboard or broken, so it is always best to be prepared.

A couple of other things should be considered when looking at tarpon rods. They should be fairly rigid with lots of backbone, particularly when your primary targets fall in the medium and large categories. It is not uncommon to have to literally lift these fish once they get close to the boat, and this is impossible with a soft, limber rod. Modern builders have developed rods with adequate lifting power as well as good castability, and this is what you should look for. In some cases, however, a rod might seem too stiff, but for giant tarpon that is almost an impossibility. If you pick up a rod and it appears to have no flexibility, chances are you won't be casting great distances for big fish, nor will you be casting all day. In fact, you will only cast when fish are spotted, making on average perhaps a dozen or so casts each trip out. For big tarpon, remember the rod is more of a fighting tool than a casting tool.

The exception is when fishing the back country for baby and small, tarpon. Here you might be a casting machine, making repeated casts into the mangroves. A rod should cast well and be easy to handle, and because the fish are small power is less important. A medium or fast action rod, one which might be used for large trout or salmon and steelhead, will work nicely.

Also, consider the guides. They should be made of heavy gauge wire because tarpon put a great deal of strain on the guides, not only during the battle but when the angler applies reverse pressure or tries to lift his prize when near the boat. Thin snake guides, such as those on many trout and salmon rods, simply won't hold up. The guides should also be large, since knots, loops and lines must travel through them freely, often at lightning speed. Ideally, the tip-top should be large as well.

Look at the reel seat and handle. The reel seat should accommodate the fly reel securely with two locking nuts. One thing you do not want is a reel coming loose during a battle with a tarpon! The handle should fit your hand comfortably and be equipped with an extension butt, a short piece of cork or rubber that extends past the end of the handle. The purpose of an extension butt is to provide a pivot when pumping the fish, or otherwise trying to control or maneuver it. Because it is positioned against the body, any extension butt should be round or have rounded edges and be made of soft material. It should not be more than two or three inches long because it might catch line during the cast or as it is being stripped out by running fish.

Another option you might want to consider, particularly if big tarpon are your primary target is a rod with a fighting foregrip. This is basically a second handle a few inches in front of the primary casting handle which provides a much more comfortable and secure hand position when applying extra leverage and lifting power. I have a 9-foot 12-weight Penn IMS tarpon rod with a foregrip and it is amazing the benefits this option provides.

There are many fine rod manufacturers today. Penn, G. Loomis, Orvis, Diamondback and St. Croix, to name a few. Look the rod over closely regardless of its name or price. If it has the features you want and feels comfortable and you like it, then it is the rod for you.

The guides on Guanaja know where to find fish, and they are warm, friendly people. The boats range from open skiffs to those with center console.

Reels

As for reels, go with the best your wallet or pocketbook can afford. Reels play a critical role in saltwater fly fishing, especially when it comes to catching tarpon, and to go cheap at this point could prove disastrous.

A tarpon reel must be ruggedly-built and able to withstand constant punishment. Perhaps the most important asset is a strong, smooth drag system, capable of releasing line under pressure with no skips and lurches. This point is critical, to have a drag start skipping when a tarpon is running away will result in something giving way, usually a knot or some other part of the leader, or the fly might rip out of the tarpon's mouth.

The reel should also accommodate at least 200 yards of 30-pound test backing. If going after big tarpon, 250 yards of backing is better I know good tarpon hunters who equip their reels with 275 or 300 yards of backing. This much backing may never be used, but at least it is there if you need it! In my personal opinion backing is more important than lots of running fly line, and it is much better to be safe than sorry. On the reels I use for big tarpon I cut off about ten feet of running line just for the purpose of adding more backing. And as I do on my reels used for bonefish and permit, I color-code the last 150 feet of backing, just so I know where I am and how much backing remains on the reel.

I also look for large drag adjustment knobs, and drags that cover a wide range during adjustment. It may be necessary to increase drag once a fish is on, and with my brain concentrating on the battle the last thing I want to do is hunt for the adjustment button. It should be large enough so the hand can easily find it. It should also cover a wide area, or increase drag gradually, taking several turns to increase pressure from low to high. If not there is a danger of over-compensating and giving too much drag, increasing the chance of breaking the fish off.

Single-action reels are strongest and most dependable. They are also the easiest to maintain and clean after use. Personally, however, I like the anti-reverse design. It allows the angler to keep a hand on the reel at all times, even when the fish is running,

The only part-time human inhabitants in Cuba's "Garden of the Queens" is a turtle research team, part of Cuba's efforts to bring back these amazing creatures. During my visit I had the opportunity to review some of the results.

and eliminates the possibility of getting knuckles or fingers whacked by the handle. It is said the drag system on anti-reverse reels is not as strong or reliable as on its single-action counterparts, but on tarpon up to 80 and 90 pounds you can't prove that to me. I have caught several on my STH Caribbean and most recently on Valentine's large Planetary reel and experienced no troubles.

As with rods, there are a lot of good reel makers out there. I have already mentioned two, STH and Valentine, but the System 2 reel by Scientific Anglers is excellent as well, retaining 80 percent of its drag force even when wet. When not using my STH or Valentines the System 2 is my reel of choice. The reels offered by Penn are wonderful, as are those by Abel, Billy Pate, Fin-Nor and Orvis, such as their new Odyssey series and DXR class, especially the anti-reverse models.

Lines

The most popular fly line for tarpon is the floater in either standard weight-forward taper, or weight-forward/saltwater taper. Much of the action for tarpon will be found in water less than five or six feet deep, and in a majority of cases sink-

ing lines aren't required. Floating lines are easier to use and perform extremely well. As for the so-called "specialty-tapers" those with names like "tarpon-taper" or "bonefish-taper," they do the job, but in most cases not enough to warrant the additional investment. If one of the specialty lines is chosen, don't spend extra money on a saltwater taper. It won't be needed.

There are times, however, when sinking below the surface with your fly line, or getting the fly deep in a hurry and keeping it there, might be required. If there is a great deal of grass and debris on the surface, which is often the case early in the season, a floating line has a way of funneling all that matter directly to the fly. In a situation like this an intermediate sinking line might be an advantage. It gets the fly just below the surface out of harm's way, yet it sinks slow and can be controlled by slowing or increasing the speed of the retrieve to work the fly at the required level. Next to the floater, this is my second choice among fly lines.

An extra fast sinking line is needed in places like the Rio Colorado in Costa Rica. In that magical place the water is thick with jungle silt. Looking much like a mud puddle after spring rains, it is impossible to see the fly soon after it hits the water, and that inland discharge continues to affect clarity far out to sea. Because of this bait swim deep, and that is where you will find tarpon, jack crevalle and the other gamesters in those rich waters. To be successful, it is necessary to get the fly down in a hurry and keep it there. An extra-fast sinking line is required, without it there is little chance of success.

Sinking lines may also be used when tarpon are deep in the passes and channels, or feeding deep along the coast. If you are rigging for a specific destination the first time and are unsure what line density is best, make a phone call to your guide, the lodge or angling booking agent and inquire. Chances are it will be a floater.

As for which brand name line is best, this is up to the angler. Cortland and Scientific Anglers lead the industry, and both are excellent. Cortland's 444SL Saltwater lines happen to be my choice at the present time because of the way they hold their "stiffness" and castability even after hours in tropical heat. The Orvis "Tropic" fly line is also very good, and comes with the front loop already attached, for those who prefer the loop-to-loop leader system.

Leaders

Perhaps the most important piece of tarpon fishing equipment is the leader. Tarpon are powerful, scrappy critters. Even the smaller ones can wreak havoc with a leader, so the connection between fly line and fly has to be strong and durable.

The standard leader system for tarpon is the shock leader, an ingenious system specifically designed for durability rather than invisibility. The butt is generally constructed of 30 or 40-pound test mono, followed by the tippet, or taper, which is made of whatever pound test material the angler desires. Eight,

An average Rio Colorado tarpon of about 70-pounds. Specimens easily reach 100 pounds and are available year-round.

ed shock leaders are also available from Orvis. In a nutshell, I like to have fun when I fish, and spend time fishing. Constructing shock leaders, at least for this angler, is not fun and takes too much time.

This does not mean the tarpon angler should not know some knots and loops. The surgeon's knot is used to attach shock tippet material to the tippet or taper, and always comes in handy. The Homer Rhode loop knot is good for attaching flies to leaders. And the double surgeon's loop is a quick, easy and strong way to put a loop in the end of a section of leader. Other than the improved clinch knot, which I sometimes use on baby tarpon, and the nail knot for attaching leaders to fly line when the loop-to-loop system isn't used, that is about it. Of course, the more knots and connections you learn the better off you will be. But again, don't worry if you never become a master.

Finally, most tarpon leaders run from 8 to 10 feet. These fish are not leader shy, however, so you don't have to go overly long. Personally, I like to keep my leaders between 8 and 8-1/2 feet. They are easy to cast, particularly under windy conditions, plus when using a 9-foot rod, which is pretty standard, the line/leader connection has less tendency to create problems going through the guides, particularly the tip-top guide.

As for other tarpon equipment and clothing, the list provided in "Section 1-Bonefish" will suffice. About the only thing you might need for tarpon, but won't need for bonefish or permit is a pair of light fishing gloves. For one thing gloves provide a better grip on the rod when playing fish. They also provide some protection from the reel, line and other items that might cut, slice or abrade the skin. Gloves should also be worn whenever handling tarpon, or when assisting in removing hooks.

A tarpon fly attached to a shock tippet. These specialized leaders can be a trial to construct, but commercial leaders make it easy.

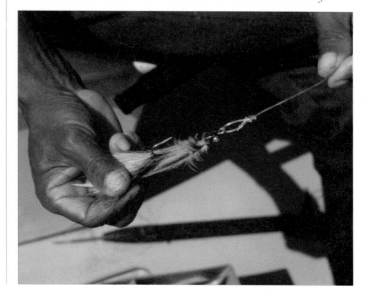

12, 16 and 20-pound test are most common. On the terminal end comes the shock tippet, a heavy piece of mono, generally in the 60 to 100-pound test range. This is assembled using the Bimini twist, surgeon's knots and loops, and it is rather impressive. Unless the angler is adept at tying these connections, it can also be a testy chore. Using *Practical Fishing Knots II* by Mark Sosin and Lefty Kreh as guides will get you started.

I will be the first to admit I am not the world's greatest knot tier. I know the basics, and tie them very well, but for me constructing a shock leader would be like tying a knot wearing ski gloves. Unless the angler is going for a specific record or is fishing alone I see no reason why the tarpon angler who fishes only occasionally should give it much concern. Independent guides in the Florida Keys and those throughout the Caribbean can generally construct shock leaders in a matter of minutes.

There is also the commercial option, which I take ninety percent of the time. As mentioned under "Section 1-Bonefish," both Umpqua and Climax offer excellent leader systems, including shock leaders in a variety of lengths and sizes. I use them religiously, and do not hesitate to recommend them. Pre-construct-

PERMIT

It is difficult to say what the good Lord was thinking when He created the family of fish classified as jacks. There are more than 35 members of this genus inhabiting North American and Caribbean waters, and though perhaps only a half dozen or so are considered viable targets on light tackle, the general philosophy of those who hunt them is that is more than enough. As a group, these six fish represent one of fly fishing's ultimate challenges, if luck and good fortune are with you and one is taken on a fly, a personal milestone has been achieved.

This is particularly true of the permit, *Trachonotus falcatus*, perhaps the most unpredictable and certainly the most elusive of the clan. To recall the times I was working a flat for bonefish and then spotting one of these desperadoes, changing flies with nervous hands and racing heart, only to be thoroughly rejected, is painful. That is the way things often go when permit is your target. You win a few, but lose more often. But those few times you win are so sweet and worth all the frustration of missed opportunities.

These fish are not easy to fool with feathers and epoxy. Each one seen can instantly elevate the human heart and soul to unparalleled heights and make the brain forget all else, just like your first love. Each refusal, and there will be many, can be totally devastating, affecting the angler in many ways long after the encounter has passed. Along with making the angler question and doubt his ability, few fish or events in skinny water can make the angler feel so inadequate.

Officially, the Atlantic permit is a member of the pompano family. This lot of rather slab-sided, snub-nosed fish also includes the familiar bar jack, the yellow-trimmed jack crevalle and amberjack. All are caught on fly rod and reel in various parts of the Caribbean, and for the untrained eye distinguishing one

Turneffe Flats in Belize is a mecca for fly anglers seeking permit which are present year-round with 40 pound fish possible.

Terry Gunn photo

from the other can be confusing. This is particularly true of the common pompano, *Trachinotus carolinus,* and juvenile permit. Both are found in shallow water as well as deep, sometimes close to shore, in bays, inlets and channels, on the flats and offshore, depending upon the season, plus they are basically identical in general appearance. Even larger fish look similar, with large pompano often mistaken for large permit, or vice versa.

There are, however, some telltale differences between the two, although for a layman it is difficult to differentiate the two in the water. Close up, the long second dorsal fin of the permit has 17 to 21 softrays, while the same dorsal on the pompano sports 22 to 27. The anal fin on permit has 16 to 19 softrays, while on the pompano there are 20 to 23, most often 21 or 22. In color, adult permit are a soft blue or gray along the back, the sides are bright silver. The dorsal fin has a dark blue, even black, front edge and the anal and pelvic fins may have an orange tinge. The largest permit are also silver, but often show a greenish-blue iridescence with dark fins. Pompano on the other hand are grayish, silver-blue, or a bluish-green along the back and upper sides, but less iridescent. The lower sides are silver or grayish as well, but typically speckled with a yellow or orange tinge, particularly near the undersides and along the breast. The same is true of the pectoral and caudal fins. The dorsal fin is a dusky or dark color.

In the water, it takes a trained and studious eye to distinguish between the two, but size is a good indicator. Pompano average around 18 inches, with large fish tipping the scales at six to eight pounds. This is considered small for permit, however, which easily reach weights into the double digits.

Permit and bonefish frequent the same areas and are often mistaken for one another, particularly when tailing or feeding

Late in the day the author's wife wades a flat on Guanaja, Bay Islands, Honduras before heading back to the lodge. The Caribbean is full of magical times and it is such moments which make a trip memorable.

with dorsal fin exposed above the water line. Early on I often confused the two, it is not uncommon for the novice to do so. Just keep in mind the caudal fins of permit are dark, often appearing black when exposed; the caudal fins of bonefish are more silvery, almost transparent. Caudal fins of permit extend higher from the water. They appear taller and much thinner. Permit are not often found in extremely shallow water where their backs are exposed. They like cover at least a foot deep, and areas where the water is from two to about four feet deep is prime territory.

Many attributes make permit the ultimate challenge, they are always on the move, always suspicious, and know exactly what they want. From an angling perspective this is a sign of a smart individual and judging from firsthand encounters I have no doubt these are intelligent fish. If not, they would be much easier to outwit with a fly, and permit are one of the most difficult fish to catch on a fly. Bonefish demand respect as do tarpon in skinny water, but these two are rather forgiving and almost easy to get on a fly in comparison. Permit are rarely easy to catch—at times they investigate an offering with a hint of interest, perhaps dallying in the immediate area as if toying with the idea of striking, perhaps they'll look over the fly several times, only to turn for some unknown reason and depart for parts unknown, leaving the angler asking "what did I do wrong this time?"

I came to the conclusion long ago that unless a major error is committed, it is nothing the angler did that makes sincere efforts go unrewarded. It is just the way permit are and is all part of the game.

There is a mystique surrounding permit that bonefish and tarpon lack. Despite being known for decades as a light tackle adversary, it is almost as if permit are shrouded in divine secrecy and refuse the angling community any great insights into their little world. For example, the most popular and productive flies for permit are those which imitate crabs, yet try as we might with variations in size and color, no matter how perfect the cast and retrieve, permit typically appear erratic and reluctant to accept artificials. The permit's mystique is only heightened when we realize that flies designed for bonefish and tarpon, and even some flies not specifically intended for them work well.

Despite numerous sightings on the flats, even on a single outing, permit are elusive and do not appear to be as numerous as bonefish and tarpon. They are rather whimsical, here one minute, gone the next. While hunting bonefish in the Bahamas and Belize I made several spottings one day, only to return the next and not spot a single one. So it goes. Experienced guides are adept at locating permit and can generally find a few even when the hunting is difficult, but there have been occasions when I invested hours in the bow of a boat poling or cruising the flats under a hot sun to no avail. During peak season, in May and again from about mid-July into September in the lower Keys and Belize, and during spring and summer months on the Yucatan, permit are much easier to find, although no less difficult to catch. Generally speaking, however, if bonefish are the "ghosts" of the flats, permit are the phantoms of the flats. And for that reason the majority of permit observed and caught are by anglers in the process of hunting for bonefish and tarpon and can sometimes be classified as coincidental. A great many of us would wish it otherwise.

This by no means lowers the desire to take these fish on a fly. In fact it only increases the desire, and permit may well be the most desired, yet seldom caught, target in skinny water. There are anglers, this writer included, who have waited and endured patiently for years for that first connection. In the meantime, one begins to wonder whether the moment will ever come.

Once hooked, response from the permit is almost instantaneous. The fact the reel starts to sing and line slices the water spraying water as it goes. It is said permit are not as fast on the run as bonefish, but I am not so sure. There have been times when my reel was well into the backing before I got a hand on the reel, and even then, the hand didn't stay long before another surge for open water.

Permit are infinitely stronger than bonefish. Their acceptance of flies may be subtle, but the subsequent runs are like hooking onto a Mack truck as it wails down the interstate. There is no stopping it, and to try would be futile. These fish also seem to possess great endurance, and unlike well played bonefish the permit's power seems inexhaustible at times, easily capable of challenging the stamina of most anglers armed with light tackle. All this considered, permit are marvelous adversaries, unquestionably the most thrilling and exciting on the flats. It is just unfortunate they come so infrequently. Then again, if they came more readily, it is doubtful they would be so esteemed, so desired and considered the ultimate shallow-water challenge.

DISTRIBUTION

Permit are the least abundant of the "big three." This reputation for scarcity may be attributed to the fact that fewer fly fishermen see them while on the flats or actually seek them out. In truth, however, the permit's natural range in the western Atlantic is actually quite extensive, and may very well exceed that of bonefish or tarpon.

Permit occur from Cape Cod, Massachusetts south to the Florida Keys, although they are considered rare north of Florida. Bermuda also has a few, although permit are not heavily sought there.

In the western Caribbean permit are quite at home from Cancun on the Yucatan Peninsula down through Belize and Honduras, undoubtedly the permit hotspots in that region. I have personally observed none while fishing for tarpon in Costa Rica, but the place is blessed with jack crevalle, which I have caught up to 40 pounds, and I have little doubt permit are present. That wonderful "Rich Coast," as Columbus called it, however, is not recommended as a viable destination for the permit hunter.

Permit are also found along the Panama shore and the South American coast all the way to Brazil. Here again, however, only one or two spots are considered serious destinations, largely due to the fact that few fishing camps exist and the availability of permit in fishable numbers has yet to be established or documented. One exception is the area around Los Roques just off Venezuela's

north coast. Even there the sighting of permit has been rated as occasional, and that lovely spot does not generally draw the serious permit enthusiast. However, those seen and many caught are large, in the 30 and 40-pound class, and for the angler traveling there it would be unwise to go without a permit rig and take advantage of any opportunities that might come along.

It is also said permit are found throughout the West Indies, but I personally observed none in Cuba, even offshore in the "Garden of the Queens." The Caymens have some, but I cannot attest to the permit status on other islands in that region, or even the Lesser Antilles. More exploring and documentation has to be done.

North of these islands, however, permit are also found in parts of the Bahamas. I spotted several on my most recent visit to Crooked Island, and several cays fished out of the North Riding Point Club on Grand Bahama are producing good catches. There is also good fishing in the Berry Islands, particularly around Hoffman Cay, Little Harbor Cay and the Fish Cays. It is not uncommon for guides to locate a permit in other locales when fishing out of established lodges as well. Some places to consider include spots around both North and South Bimini, Gun Cay, North and South Cat Cays and Victory Cay, all south of South Bimini. The west side

Other species are available on Caribbean flats. Barracuda and various jacks, like this small reef jack, can be taken on flies. The author's wife, Diane took this fish on a six-weight outfit and it proved to be great fun.

of Andros has permit, as does Cat Island, 130 miles southeast of Nassau. It should be pointed out, however, while permit exist in the Bahamas and are caught there it is bonefish which keep them on the angling map. Few lodges advertise for them, as yet permit are not considered a prime target, nor are the Bahamas a major permit destination.

Without question the best permit opportunities are found in the Florida Keys, particularly around Key West; some of the largest permit are taken there year after year, and in the western Caribbean region from the Yucatan south to Belize and Honduras. The fishing in each of these areas is consistently good, both in terms of numbers of fish, size and catchability. Spots in the Yucatan, and Belize in particular, offer the best chance for a "Grand Slam", the unique distinction of taking a bonefish, tarpon and permit on the same day.

LIFE CYCLE

Much research remains to be done about the permit's life cycle. As it is with bonefish and tarpon, information concerning their early years and how long they live continues to be speculative and vague. It is known permit spawn offshore in the deep blue. Late spring seems to be the most accepted spawning period around south Florida, most probably in late May through June since inshore numbers seem to drop off about that time. Some of the best action during this period is found near deep water reefs and wrecks, and it is reported males and females are full of milt or eggs at that time. Elsewhere the spawning season may extend from December to early fall, depending upon the locale.

When the newborns reach a length of about 1-1/2 to 2 inches they slowly navigate toward shore. There they remain and grow, moving in and out with the seasons just like adults. Little is known about growth rates, but fish of just two or three pounds contribute to the sports fishery. Traveling in schools from just a few to several dozen, juvenile permit are roundish, turning more oblong with age. Older permit also seem to be more solitary, traveling in pairs, or groups of three.

From an angling perspective, these are the fish you want. The chance for success seems to increase with those solitary adults that are away from the main school. Compared to bonefish and tarpon, my success ratio with permit is not good, but those I caught were either singles or in pairs. Whether or not this is always the case or mere coincidence I cannot say, but investing a great deal of time casting to permit found in groups does not appear to be extremely productive.

SIZE

Any permit spotted and observed in skinny water is impressive, an inspiration regardless of size. The fact they are not easily caught, the need for respect when casting to them, or their power once hooked, may all be contributing factors. A permit is like no

An experimental dolphin station is located near Turtle Cay, east of Abaco, Bahamas. Shows are open to the public.

other gamester, and size has little to do with it. The biggest permit I have set eyes on was meticulously working a coral flat near the island of Guanaja, one of the Bay Islands of Honduras, a good permit hotspot. Our guide, a young and knowledgeable local by the name of Carmen, excitedly estimated the giant at 35 to 40 pounds, and by his actions I guessed it was one of the biggest he had ever seen as well. On the other end of the scale I have observed, and cast to permit barely making 10 pounds by my estimates, yet they also aroused my interest and I was as captivated by them as much as I was their larger counterparts.

Permit up to 50 pounds have been caught. Fish of this size are not common and those in the 30 pound range are considered trophies.

The majority of permit taken on fly rod throughout the Caribbean run between 15 and 25 pounds. In the lower Florida Keys, which are known for producing some of the largest permit, the average may be slightly higher, but timing is critical. The Keys are also the best bet for finding large permit over 40 pounds. Yucatan and Belize produce some big permit, too and also Honduras, Venezuela and at some locales in the Bahamas.

WATER TEMPERATURES AND SEASONS

Permit are extremely sensitive to cold water temperatures. They are the least cold-tolerant of the "Big Three." It is rare to

consistently find them in skinny water when temperatures are below 72-degrees, and it has been observed that when temperatures fall below this mark they evacuate the flats. Their preferred temperature range is roughly between 74 and 84-degrees. Permit will be found where water is slightly warmer, although once temperatures get higher than 86 or 87-degrees they move to deeper water.

The further south you travel the better your chances of finding permit for longer periods of time, if not year-round. A few permit can always be found around Los Roques in Venezuela, and according to guides working out of the Posada Del Sol Resort on the island of Guanaja just off the coast of Honduras, permit are a permanent fixture. The same is true in areas fished by Belize River Lodge and Turneffe Flats, both in Belize. Further north on the Yucatan, permit are also available year around, and good fishing is always possible, but April through August is generally considered prime. As elsewhere in the western Caribbean and down through Central America, August and September are the hurricane months, and in some spots the rainy season. Some flats may become unfishable due to high tides or muddy water being washed into the sea.

In the Florida Keys, particularly that stretch from Big Pine Key down to Key West and through the Marquesas, permit start to show in February. Cold fronts and dropping water temperatures make the angling unpredictable in March; April and May are generally considered the prime spring months. There is good fishing in June, especially in deeper water around wrecks and reefs, but based on personal experience better opportunities are found in July and August. Permit remain available right into fall until cold temperatures push them again to deeper areas.

In general, April, May and June, and September and October, are the best periods to hunt permit depending upon the location. This is true in the Bahamas, but like everything else in life, there are exceptions. Some areas offer permit for short periods, like those flats north of Cancun on the Yucatan which are only productive from about late April through July; some are productive for longer periods, during spring, summer and early fall, like the Florida Keys, while other places are fortunate to offer them year-round, like Belize and Honduras. Even in some "year-round" destinations, however, like spots in Mexico and the Yucatan, there are peak periods, basically May through August.

Because of these variables nothing beats personal research. If permit are the objective do your homework before booking a date. Contact a guide specializing in permit, such as Marshall Cutchin in Key West, or a booking agent like Doug Schlink or Chip Bates at Angler Adventures, John Eustice of John Eustice Associates representing lodges and camps, or a lodge operator, like Craig Hayes of Turneffe Flats, where permit are a primary target, and pick their brains. These reputable guides, agents and lodge operators, and others like them, know when and where to fish their areas best.

FOOD AND FLIES

When it comes to food. Permit are somewhat more selective than tarpon and bonefish, although permit will nail small baitfish on occasion, their primary culinary desire includes crabs and shrimp. This includes common blue crabs, green reef crabs, mud and stone crabs, snapping shrimp, mantis shrimp and mud shrimp, among others. Flies which imitate these marine animals should be readily available.

Fly selection goes much further than just having a few crab and shrimp patterns. Color, size and a general idea in what geographic area and type of habitat each natural is found all play a roll. Some crabs are most common on muddy bottoms, others are only found on grass flats or sandy bottoms. Still others are found in shallow water on sandy bottoms around mangroves or oyster beds. Some species are found throughout the Caribbean, south Florida and Bahamas, while others have a smaller geographic range.

Crabs are also different in color and size. Some are bluish-gray like the blue crab. This is a common crab in Florida, the Bahamas, Belize and Honduras. The green reef crab, common in Florida, the Caribbean and Bahamas is a medium green, sometimes dark green. Others are brownish, white, cream or yellow in color. They may vary from under an inch to two or three inches in size, and trying to match the relative size of the natural can be as important as approximating the color.

Whatever colors the crabs may be, to increase your chances of success it helps to know the type of bottom in the area you will be fishing. Some species aren't found on muddy bottoms, others won't be found where there is a great deal of grass or coral. If possible find out the color and most common size of the crab population. Of course, a good many guides, lodge owners and booking agents will take the easy route and just recommend fly patterns and hook sizes that work in the given area. That is perfectly acceptable, since that is really what we want to know anyway. But on the trip, particularly if you tie your own flies, keep an observant eye and take notes. That way you can experimenting and perhaps be better prepared for the next visit.

There are, however, a number of popular and productive crab flies available that have become standards whenever and wherever permit are sought. If I had to pick just two that short list would include the Del Brown Permit Fly, a brownish/tan offering with white legs tipped in red, in size 1/0. Completing the set would by George Anderson's, McCrab, in size 2 to 1/0. Both are available commercially by Umpqua Feather Merchants and can be found at tackle and fly shops in the Keys, on some islands in the Bahamas and through mail order from many saltwater angling outlets. It is not unusual for many lodges in the Caribbean with fly shops to also carry them.

These are not, however, the only crab imitations worth considering. Tim Borski's, Chernobyl Crab is a good one, sizes 1/0 to 2, as is Captain Lenny Moffo's, Green Antron Crab. The Turneffe Crab, created by Craig Mathews and available in brown, cream, green and olive in sizes 4 to 8 is good wherever small crabs are predominant. These and other crab imitations are mentioned and listed in several fly tying books, including *Saltwater Flies* by Deke Meyer; *Flies for Saltwater* by Dick Stewart and Farrow Allen and "Saltwater *Fly Patterns*" by Lefty Kreh.

As for shrimp offerings, many of the fly patterns normally associated with bonefish also produce permit. Captain Nat Ragland's Puff Fly has been known to take a permit now and then, and has arguably produced more permit over the years than any other crab fly. A list of popular and productive bonefish flies is listed in "BONEFISH" under "Food and Flies." I wouldn't hesitate to use any of them, particularly if working for bones and a permit is spotted, which often happens. Normally, heavier leaders are used for permit, but don't pass up the opportunity if it knocks. You might be surprised, and have nothing to lose.

Permit are a primary target at Posada del Sol, Honduras. Permit are available year-round, and it is not uncommon to see a dozen or more each day. This one was caught by the author's wife, Diane, her first!

SPOTTING PERMIT

Over the years I have seen fewer permit, to say nothing of catching far less, but the art of spotting has not been as difficult to learn with permit than it has for bonefish. I still do not claim to be a master of that craft, and I hope the day never comes when each trip out fails to reveal something new, but for me permit just make themselves known a whole lot easier.

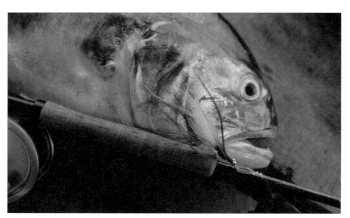

A small jack crevalle taken by the author on a red and yellow whistler. Even small jacks are a joy.

Perhaps their size has something to do with it. These are deep, slab-sided critters and their form takes up more area, they often appear more ghostlike below the surface. Permit are rarely still. Even when searching for something to eat they are in perpetual motion.

But the most telltale sign of their presence is the permit's dorsal fin. Tall, sickle-shaped and black it often sticks above the water line, it is the neophyte's best hope of easily spotting these fish. There are times, particularly when wading, when a permit is almost on top of the angler before seen. They have an uncanny ability to appear out of nowhere, and the first thing spotted is often the black dorsal protruding above and slicing the water's surface.

Considering their size and great depth permit are generally found in deeper water than bonefish. They like to keep their backs covered and though I have observed permit in water a foot deep, it has not been very often. Water from two to perhaps four feet deep seems to be the preferred working area when on the flats. Permit seem to arrive on a flat later than bonefish. Again, this is undoubtedly due to their size and depth which simply requires more water to get up on the flats. This is why on some small flats, which may be shallow at other times, permit fishing is only productive on the incoming or high tide. Look for them on the outside edges of flats, where shallow water tapers off to deep, on the edge of channels cutting through two flats, anywhere the water is knee deep or slightly more. When the tide is right, permit may be found close to shore on the inside of a flat, even right up on a flat, but more times than not they will be seen closer to deeper, open water. Often permit are not spotted by unguided hunters because they are working in water that is too shallow, or during the wrong time of tide.

Permit seem to prefer specific bottom types. They like rock and coral areas where there are depressions, pockets and rock formations in which crabs and shrimp can hide. I have only caught one permit where turtle grass was abundant, but overall I have seen few permit in that type cover. Whether this is characteristic or just circumstance I cannot say. Judging by the fact that grassy flats are utilized by bonefish, I would think permit frequent such areas on the right tides as well, considering the rich store of food stuffs, including crabs, shrimp and small baitfish.

Finally, unlike bonefish, permit do not create a "mud" while feeding. However, they are often found close to these areas, or spotted investigating a mud while looking for leftover morsels. When a mud is discovered, don't be quick to leave.

CASTING, RETRIEVING, HOOKING AND PLAYING PERMIT

Casting to bonefish on the flats is a challenge that has been heralded as one of fly fishing's great tests with a fly rod, and few who have taken up that challenge would disagree. But permit are something else again. On a scale of one to ten, if casting to bonefish is a five or six, casting to permit is at least a ten, if not off the scale altogether. Just making a successful cast to one of these fish is a supreme challenge.

Presentation and retrieve have to be precise to get a permit's attention, to say nothing of getting one to strike. That in itself is nothing short of a miracle, or so it seems. Many permit hunters get excited when they see one of these fish, and in that excitement commit mistakes which cannot be reversed. Remain cool, calm and collected. It is imperative to challenge permit with a clear head and a plan when possible. Sometimes permit appear out of nowhere, they may be on the move and provide little time for thought, but when that happens I have found it best to remain still, low to the water and bide my time. I have had permit travel within 20 or 30 feet of me and never spook. There is always a greater risk of failure working to a permit on the move, and to do so is almost always an attempt in futility.

The fish you want is one that is feeding since it will have its mind on something else, its head down so its chances of seeing you will be reduced. The fish may be moving slowly, as if hunting, but ideally it should be stopped and probing the bottom. If the permit is moving, again, do not move or make a cast until it has stopped to occupy itself. Stay put and try to determine which direction it is moving. Chances are it will be moving into the tide, so a position above and slightly to the side is preferred. This will reduce the chance of kicking up sand and marl, having it drift downstream and warning the permit of your presence. It will also provide an opportunity to cast at an angle to the fish, rather than straight on. This reduces the chances of over-casting your target, keeps the fly line away from the permit, and makes it easier to achieve greater accuracy, a major key in determining success.

When ready to cast, remember the permit must first see what is being offered. The fly can be dropped well ahead of the permit by six to eight feet and then be gently worked until it is seen. This is the safest alternative, since a fly hitting the water further away has less chance of creating a disturbance and spooking the permit. It is not, however, the most productive method, and among many experienced hunters leading a permit this way is only done when a fish is spotted cruising and no other option is possible.

When permit are feeding, the best tactic is to drop the fly as close to the fish as possible, ideally within two or three feet of the nose. There is a great threat of creating disturbance and alarming

the permit of course, but there is no way around it and this is a chance the angler must take. If possible, wait until the permit seems consumed in its foraging, perhaps even with its back to you, before making the cast. Work with a slightly open loop in your cast, and aim to an imaginary point six or seven feet above the water. Allow the fly to drop to the water gently. Remember, if casting a crab, they are bottom dwellers, and that is where your permit will be looking. Allow sufficient time, with any cast, for the offering to get to the bottom.

Once the cast has been made, the next move is no move at all. It breaks every rule about fly retrieval we have ever held dear, but allow the fly to sit. Our intention is to imitate a crab, and when a crab sees a permit, or vice versa it holds its ground. Fleeing would be futile making the crab a much easier and more vulnerable target. Your fly should do the same thing. Only if the permit turns away, as if not interested, should it be moved. Doing so will often cause the permit to turn for another look, if that happens the fly should be immediately stopped again. If casting to a permit on the move, it is often necessary to retrieve the fly until it gets into proper position, or until the permits sees it, but make sure the fly is on the bottom when the permit closes in for a look.

Your fly rod should be level with the water at this point, or pointed slightly downward, and the line should be slack-free. Keep the fly still as long as the permit is grubbing around, moving it only when you feel the permit take it. Gently lift the rod tip up and to the side, if resistance is felt continue the sweep to the side. It is not necessary to strike these fish with the tenacity used on tarpon. The permit's mouth is softer, more like soft rubber or leather, and the up-and-to-the-side sweep of the rod, plus the fish's movement is enough to set the hook. Generally permit only provide one opportunity, but if no resistance is felt, immediately drop the rod tip. This will send the fly back to the bottom, and if the permit is still around, might draw another look.

If a connection is made, the angler soon knows it. Permit make a speedy retreat once hooked that can test any reel and drag. There is no way to stop these fish on the run, and to try will only result in something giving way, either the hook, leader or a knot. On the initial run I generally have my drag set with only enough tension to prevent a backlash of line and put minimal pressure on the fish. The fish will feel increasing pressure as more and more line is being stripped from the reel. Too much tension from the drag increases pressure too quickly on these sizzling runs, and all to often the fish is lost. Allow it to run, increasing drag gradually as the fish slows, taking in line whenever possible. Trying to over-power a permit until it begins to tire greatly increases the chance of losing it, so enjoy the moment. The battle with these fish is not easily won, and victory is more often achieved by the angler who uses brains over brawn. Use all the power the tackle and situation will allow, but use it wisely. This is especially true as the battle comes to an end and the permit gets in close. Permit are known to make sudden runs even when it appearing tired. If the permit moves left, lower the rod and power to the right. If it moves to the right, power left.

Another test comes when the battle is finally over. When wading, permit can be tailed and gently lifted from the water, but no attempt should be made until the fish is spent and can be maneuvered easily into position. When that time comes and the permit is within reach firmly grip the caudal peduncle as close to the tail as possible, and lift, being cautious of the secondary spiny dorsal tail. It is not a bad idea to wear a pair of gloves, which not only protect the hands but provide a firmer, more secure hold on the fish. By lifting the permit in this matter it is thrown off balance and will hang there and allow the fly to be removed, yet it does no harm. Permit may also be netted, and I have seen some gaffed, but when tailing is possible, neither is a viable option.

Never put your fingers inside the mouth of a permit. These fish are equipped with a set of crushers which can do damage. Use a pair of long-nosed pliers or forceps to remove the hook. Finally, when releasing permit, give them plenty of time to recuperate fully before letting them go. They fight with all their heart and will literally battle until totally spent, so make sure they swim off on their own power.

EQUIPMENT

A great many permit are taken on the same equipment used for bonefish (see page 26). This consists normally of a 9-foot rod designed for size 7 or 8 line equipped with a suitable reel, 200 to 250 yards of backing and a floating standard weight-forward or saltwater taper line. Standard bonefish leaders, those from 9 to 12 feet or so with six or eight pound test tippets, will suffice, but it will be necessary to use some patience and diligence, particularly when a sizzling run is made or when the permit uses its vertical depth to its advantage.

When specifically hunting permit, however, you might want to consider a heavier outfit, something in the 9 or 10-weight class. The heavier kit will make handling and playing these fish a lot easier. Permit are also masters at heading for the bottom and using whatever is available to dislodge the fly. For that reason, I generally use heavier leaders, as well, typically 10 or 12-pound test tippets.

Hummingbirds are a common sight at Posada del Sol while dining on the open veranda.

DESTINATIONS

The Caribbean basin, including the Bahamas and south Florida, are full of wondrous and enchanting places to pursue bonefish, tarpon and permit. A person could spend a lifetime in the Bahamas alone, and still not fish every flat, or see all there is to see.

I have been extremely fortunate to visit and explore many places within the Caribbean. Each one is a fond memory, and each has left its mark on mind and soul which keeps drawing me back. Some of the places I consider to be among the best when it comes to providing world class fly fishing for "the Big Three," are covered here. We will take a look at what they have to offer the angler, including their history and other aspects which make them truly unique.

THE BAHAMAS

A mere 50 miles off Florida's east coast, the unique archipelago that is the Bahamas begins. Starting with Grand Bahama and Abaco on the north this extensive chain of islands and cays stretches to Great Inagua, almost at the doorstep of Haiti and the Dominican Republic, more than 600 miles to the southeast. As a whole the Bahamas consist of more than 700 low-lying islands and over 2,400 cays. The total land mass is about 5,400-square miles, slightly more than Connecticut and Rhode Island combined. Interestingly, only about fifteen of the larger islands have been developed to any degree. Many islands are populated, but many more are not. And there are vast parts of the Bahamas which represent genuine wilderness. Indeed, there are places where the angler can totally escape the hustle and bustle of the modern world. That is part of the charm, the great attraction, that is the Bahamas. All things considered, there is no other place on earth quite like it.

Belize River Lodge is located on the mainland, just a few minutes drive from the international airport. Surrounded by a beautifully landscaped yard, the lodge offers all the amenities of home.

Brian O'Keefe photo

In fact, many islands have changed little since Columbus first arrived on what is now San Salvador in October of 1492. The lower Bahamas were populated by Arawak Indians then, primitive farmers and fishermen who would see their world and way of life come to an unfortunate end within a few short decades. Today, no descendants of the Arawak people survive. The islands were claimed by the British in 1629, and actually received their first constitution that year as part of the Carolinas. There is a rich history of pirating and buccaneering surrounding the Bahamas, and the islands became a haven for high sea lawlessness. Old forts and strongholds, some complete with cannons, still exist. One exists near Landrail Point on the northern tip of Crooked Island, and can be explored by visiting fishermen. Other than minor disputes over ownership, the Bahamas remained under British control until 1973, when it became independent, within the Commonwealth.

Today, the Bahamas is a place of peace and order. It is safe to visit and travel, but with tourism contributing more than 70 percent of the country's income, there is a hectic hustle and bustle on the more developed islands and in larger towns, so always take precautions with valuables. This is primarily true in Nassau and Freeport. On the smaller islands I have never felt anything but completely safe and welcome and have found the Bahamian people as a whole to be some of the warmest and friendliest anywhere.

The interesting thing about the Bahamas is it is almost two separate worlds. The northern islands, Abaco, Grand Bahama, Andros, Eleuthera and New Providence, for example, are the most developed and populated. For the most part, these are the Bahamas that tourists and anglers are familiar with, yet to the

southeast is a largely undeveloped fly fishing utopia waiting to be explored. Extensive bonefish flats, some of the best in the world, will be found around these islands, particularly Grand Bahama, Abaco, the Berry Islands, Andros and the Exumas, but these are only a part of what the Bahamas has to offer. It is estimated over 70,000 square miles of shoal water surround these islands, representing the most extensive bonefish flats on the planet.

A good portion of it can be found around the central and southern islands. This is the other Bahamas. There are fewer large towns and fewer people, and they are more difficult to reach. Neon lights don't exist except in a bar, and fishing resorts and guides are few. But the angling opportunities around Crooked Island, the Acklins and South Andros, even the Turks and Caicos far to the south, offer a bonefish paradise the angling world has yet to discover. For the person looking to get away from it all and do some exploring these islands should not be overlooked. There are places which literally have yet to see a fly.

One final note. Getting to the Bahamas can be as easy as making a reservation and getting on a plane and flying to Nassau or Freeport. Even some of the smaller towns such as Marsh Harbor on Abaco and Bimini can be reached direct from Miami. The problems, however, begin when traveling to some of the outer islands. Bahamas Air is the primary inter-island carrier, and while they do a good job, they have been known to overbook and, leave or arrive early or late causing a lot of problems for someone on a schedule. Lost baggage can be another problem, even when traveling from or making connections in Miami. You will discover this is nothing unusual in the Bahamas. Book your flight early, confirm tickets and arrive at the airport well before departure. Flight insurance is highly advised in the Bahamas.

If traveling to the outer islands it might be to your advantage to use a private charter, particularly in light of the fact that many fishing resorts have their own air strip, and clients can be delivered almost to the doorstep. It may cost more, but with three or four fishermen in a group, not a great deal more, plus it is quick, easy and you get to your destination when you want. On my last trip I flew from Treasure Cay on Abaco to Caribe Bay Resort at Landrail Point on Crooked Island with Larry Meredith, (New Bight, Cat Island, Telephone: 809-342-3018). If possible this is the only way to go when visiting the smaller, more isolated islands and time is a factor. Even when traveling commercial carriers, keep baggage to a minimum. Charter services, and Bahamas Air especially, have a weight limit of 40 pounds per person.

1) BONEFISH BAY CAMP

Location: Kemps Bay, South Andros Island
Capacity/Lodge Size: 6 to 8 fishermen
Travel Itinerary: Nassau to Congotown via Congo Air, transfer to Bonefish Bay Camp. Private charter directly to Congotown
Accommodations: Air conditioned rooms, mini refrigerators, private bath, double beds, television, all linens, daily maid service and laundry service. The camp does not sell liquor or beer. Bottled water and soft drinks stocked in room refrigerators.
Primary Game fish: Bonefish (some permit are seen but are not numerous)
Size: 3 to 5 pound average, and plentiful; larger fish a good possibility
Distance to Flats: 10 to 20 minutes
Flats-Type: Mostly white sand, some coral and grass
Fishing Available: Most fishing is done by wading, some from boats
Boats/Motors: Guided Rahming bonefishing skiffs/50hp out boards

2) CARIBE BAY RESORT

Location: Landrail Point, Crooked Island
Capacity: 16 rooms, each double occupancy
Travel Itinerary: Nassau to Pittstown, Crooked Island via Bahamas Air on Tuesdays and Saturdays, ground transfer to Landrail Point. Private charter directly to Caribe Bay Resort at Landrail Point
Accommodations: 4-plex detached sleeping building, private bath/shower, ceiling fans, private verandahs. Dining room and bar. Drinks and beer in the bar are reasonably priced
Primary Fish: Bonefish, with some permit possible
Size: 2 to 5 pound average. Large fish up to 10 pounds possible
Distance to Best Flats: 45 to 90 minutes
Flats-Type: Primarily white sand and grass some of the finest wading in the Bahamas
Boats/Motors: Non-typical flats boats, but great for travel to and from the flats nearly all fishing is done by wading
Fishing Available: Nearly all by wading
Areas Fished: Areas around Long Cay, Fish Cay, Guana Cay, the Acklins, Ratland Goat Cays, French Wells
Notes: Crooked Island is remote, but it is one of the loveliest spots in the Bahamas. The area is home to thousands of bonefish, many of which are found in large schools. Fish can be difficult to find at times, but when located some consistently productive action is possible. Scott Heywood reports taking several dozen fish a day.

Although I haven't faired as well, the fishing is good. The guides, led by head guide Elton McKinney, and Kirk McKinney, are not well versed in fly fishing, but they know how to locate fish and are good spotters. The accommodations are good, and the beer is always cold!

3) NORTH RIDING POINT CLUB

Location: Grand Bahama Island, 20 minutes from Freeport

Capacity: See "Notes" below

Travel Itinerary: Freeport, GBI, via ground transport to resort

Accommodations: Large bedrooms, main dining room, bar, airy verandahs, fly tying room. See "Notes" below

Primary Fish: Bonefish. Tarpon are also in the area around Sale Cay, as well as a fair number of permit. Not necessarily a great place for a grand slam, but the possibility certainly exists. One of the few places in the Bahamas where bonefish, tarpon and permit are actually pursued.

Size: Bonefish; 4 to 6 pound average, 8 to 10-pounders quite possible. Tarpon; 40 to 60 pound average, larger examples possible. Permit; 10 to 20 pound average, larger fish possible

Distance to Flats: Boats are trailered to different areas for launching. Actual boat time to flats varies, but generally under 30 minutes

Flats-Type: White sand, some soft bottom, some grass

Boats/Motors: Specially designed Dolphin skiffs, each equipped with seats ahead of the console, stainless steel thigh brace on casting platform and a cowling around the casting platform to keep line from blowing off the deck. Full time mechanic on duty

Fishing Available: Wading and from boats

Areas Fished: Hall's Point, Cross Cays, South East Point, Sale Cay, Water Cay, Mangrove Cay and others

Notes: North Riding Point Club was still under construction in the spring of 1995. Opening date is Fall/1995. Planned as one of the premier fishing resorts in the Bahamas, and once complete there is little doubt it will achieve that goal. The owners are Ed and Carol Dawes. Both have years of experience in running a bonefish lodge and are well known among Bahama fly fishermen. Testimony to that fact is the lovely, meticulously planned lodge currently being built, attention given to details which can make or break a trip, and the hiring of top guides like Stanley Glinton. Stanley has some 25 years as a guide at the Deep Water Cay Club, and will serve as North Riding Point's head guide.

4) SANDY POINT/OEISHA'S RESORT

Location: Sandy Point, Great Abaco Island

Capacity: 6 to 10 fishermen

Travel Itinerary: Commercial flight—US Air, American Eagle— to Marsh Harbor, Great Abaco Island. Over-land drive to Sandy Point. Private charter flight from Marsh Harbor to Sandy Point

Accommodations: Double occupancy air conditioned rooms in a villa-type setting. Private bath/shower, television. Main dining room and bar.

Primary Fish: Bonefish, permit are also available

Size: 3 to 6 pound average. Larger examples into double digits not uncommon and quite possible, especially from October through March. Permit, under 20 pounds on average. However, larger fish, some up to 40 pounds are often seen from October to early December. In season, Sandy Point is a great place to catch BIG permit

Distance to Flats: 20 to 60 minutes

Flats-Type: Hard bottom white sand, some soft bottom, some grass. Many flats are quite extensive and, compared to other destinations in the Bahamas, are under-fished

Boats/Motors: Flats-style boats and non-flats-style boats

Fishing Available: Primarily wading, but also from boats in some locales

Areas Fished: Areas of Gorda Cay, Mores Island and flats close to Sandy Point

Notes: Sandy Point/Oeisha's Resort is one of those great get-away Bahama destinations that is relatively easy to reach. The lodge is located close to the village of Sandy Point, a quiet, friendly settlement with a general store and other services. Bonefish numbers are excellent, and compared to other areas they are not overly sophisticated, nor are they easy. October, November and early December are excellent months for large bones and permit, although there is a chance for a late hurricane or some cool weather. The winter months, mid-December through March produce big bonefish, but the weather is variable and sometimes cool, cloudy, windy with rain possible. April, May and June bring warming waters and calming winds and large schools of bones; July through September is the classic "tailing time," particularly early and late in the day. Sandy Point/Oeisha's Resort is owned by Earnist Flowers, a gentle giant of a man who will go out of his way to make your trip enjoyable as well as a success. Patrick Roberts is the head guide, a local who knows area waters and flats like the back of his hand, and an able fly fisherman in his own right.

5) TREASURE CAY/COOPERSTOWN AREA

Location: North end of Great Abaco Island

Travel Itinerary: Commercial carrier to Marsh Harbor or Treasure Cay Airport, ground transport to Treasure Cay

Accommodation: 4 to 6 fishermen/2 couples in condominium at Treasure Cay Resort. Two condos are available. Each is air conditioned with cable television, full modern bath and laundry room, electric stove and refrigerator, microwave oven and other conveniences

Primary Fish: Bonefish

Size: 2 to 6 pounds average. Larger examples in the 8 pound class quite possible and not unusual. Bonefish into double digits a good possibility

Distance to Flats: Fishermen are met and picked up at the condo by guides and travel by vehicle to launch area. Driving time is approximately 20 to 60 minutes. Boat time to flats may be from 10 minutes to as much as one hour

Flats-Type: Hard bottom, soft bottom and some grass

Boats and Motors: Typical flats-style fishing boats

Fishing Available: Wading and by boat, depending upon area fished

Areas Fished: The extensive flats near Cooperstown, including those near Randall's Cay, Rocky Harbor Cay, Basin Harbor Cay, Cave Cay, Cross Cay, and Daniel's and Smith Cays. The northern end of the fabulous "marls" are also fished. This is a remote area of mangrove and shallow flats which stretch almost 70 miles south towards Sandy Point. This is one of my favorite bonefish hotspots in the Bahamas. I have landed up to 20 bones in the marls in a single day, and I took my largest-ever bonefish there as well. The fish measured 31 inches from nose to fork, and weighed an estimated 11 to 12 pounds. I have yet to equal it anywhere

Notes: This is a perfect fishing/vacation trip for couples or families, considering the luxurious accommodations and do-it-yourself-style amenities. Non-fishing party members can enjoy nearby restaurants, shops, tennis, golf, snorkeling and the powder-soft, three-mile-long beach. The fishing, however, is some of the best, whether in the marls or north around Cooperstown. The guides are some of the best as well, including O'Donald McIntosh, one of the premier Bahamian guides.

6) SOUTH ANDROS BONEFISH LODGE

Location: Kemp's Bay, South Andros Island

Travel Itinerary: Commercial carrier to Nassau, then CongoAir to Congotown. Several small international carriers also provide daily service between Miami and Congotown. The lodge is just a 15-minute drive from Congotown Airport

Accommodations: 8 fishermen. Lodging is in a century-old private home nestled into Kemp's Bay. Surrounded by palms and a white sandy beach this is a beautiful spot. Guest rooms, bath rooms and social areas are simple, but the lodge is spotlessly clean and spacious. Meals are provided, and served on a delightful screened-in porch overlooking the tongue of the ocean

Primary Fish: Bonefish

Size: 3 to 6 pound average. Larger examples often seen and are quite possible

Distance to Flats: 10 to 20 minutes, some longer

Flats-Type: Hard white sand, some soft bottom and some grass

Boats/Motors: 16 to 18-foot custom-designed flats-style boats/30-50hp Mercury outboards

Fishing Available: Most of the fishing is by wading, but boats are also used in some areas

Additional information and booking arrangements for Destinations 1 through 6 may be obtained by contacting: *Angling Destinations,* 330 N. Main Street, Sheridan, WY. 82801, Telephone: 307-672-6894 or 1-800-211-8530.

7) ANDROS ISLAND BONEFISH CLUB

Location: Andros Island, at the confluence of Cargill Creek, the Atlantic Ocean and North Bight

Travel Itinerary: Commercial carrier (Gulfstream Air) from Miami to Andros Town. Gulfstream Air frequently runs late, so be prepared. Ground transfer from airport to lodge, approximately 35 minutes

Accommodations: 28 fishermen. Constructed in 1967, renovated in 1992. Rooms are air conditioned with ceiling fans, dressers and closets. Several rooms have satellite television. Housekeeping service, laundry service. The spacious lounge and bar area, and dining room overlook the water

Primary Fish: Bonefish, permit, tarpon

Size: Bonefish 3 to 5 pound average. Larger fish available and quite common. Permit 8 to 12 pound average, but 40 pound permits have been caught. Tarpon up to 100 pounds, examples 50 to 60 pounds average

Distance to Flats: From just in front of lodge to approximately one hour

Flats-Type: Hard-packed sand, some soft sand area and grass areas

Boats/Motors: Typical flats-style skiffs

Fishing Available: Most of the fishing is by wading, with many flats reached by boat. Fishing is also from boats in some areas

Areas Fished: Flats immediately close to the lodge. Other areas include flats around Big Wood Cay between North and Middle Bight; White Bight, Young Sound, Moxey Creek and Behring Point; Big Loggerhead Creek, Little Loggerhead Creek, Cabbage Creek, Miller Creek and Little Miller Creek. The guides also have places fished regularly that they call "Land of the Giants," "Bonefish Boulevard," "Soft Mud Bight" and "The Promised Land."

Notes: Andros Island Bonefish Club is one of the premier angling destinations in the Bahamas. Owner Rupert Leadon lives on the property, has been in business for years and knows how to run a top-notch fishing lodge. The guides are experienced, friendly and know the area waters intimately.

8) CARGILL CREEK LODGE

Location: Andros Island, at the mouth of Cargill Creek, the Atlantic ocean and eastern end of North Bight

Capacity: 30 fishermen

Travel Itinerary: Gulfstream Air from Miami to Andros Town, 35 minutes taxi to lodge

Accommodations: Four single rooms, seven double rooms and three villas each having two bedrooms and two baths. All rooms are air conditioned with ceiling fans. Daily housekeeping, lounge, full service bar and spacious dining room. Freshwater swimming pool.

Primary Fish: Bonefish, tarpon, permit

Size: Bonefish 3 to 5 pound average, larger examples often taken. Tarpon 40 to 60 pounds average, examples up to 100 pounds possible. Permit 8 to 12 pounds average, 40 pound fish possible

Distance to Flats: Flats are located almost in front of the lodge, others require an hour boat ride

Boats/Motors: Typical flats-type skiffs, some equipped with poling platforms

Fishing Available: Wading and from boats

Areas Fished: See Andros Island Bonefish Club

Notes: Cargill Creek Creel Lodge is a world-class fishing retreat and one of the best known in the Bahamas. It is a great spot for fishermen, as well as non-fishing partners.

9) GRASSY CAYS CAMP

Location: Grassy Cay, 70 miles south of Cargill Creek Lodge

Capacity: Contact booking agent

Travel Itinerary: Grassy Cays Camp is owned and operated by Cargill Creek Lodge. The travel itinerary is the same, except a 70 mile boat ride from Cargill Creek is required to reach the lodge. Travel time is approximately two hours. The smoothness of the ride depends upon the weather, and fishermen should have raingear available as well as water repellent covers for their luggage

Accommodations: Double occupancy air conditioned rooms, dining area, bar, bathroom/shower, generated power. The island has its own freshwater supply

Primary Fish: Bonefish, tarpon and permit

Size: Bonefish run 2-6-pound average, but examples in double digits are not rare. Permit run 10 to 20 pound average, with larger specimens possible. Tarpon 40 to 60 pound average, although tarpon up to 80 and 90 pounds have been taken. Larger tarpon possible

Distance to Flats: Flats are located within walking distance of the lodge, and may be fished solo after the guides have left for the day. Many flats are within 20 or 30 minutes of the lodge; some are further away

Flats-Type: Extensive white hard sand, some soft sand, and grass

Boats/Motors: Rahming-style flats skiffs, many equipped with poling platforms/40hp outboards

Fishing Available: A great deal of wading and some by boats

Areas Fished: Many of the flats around Grassy Cay are nameless, but the opportunities are limitless

Notes: Grassy Cay is a new destination as of 1994. Due to its location and access, this is a trip for the adventurous, but the area offers some of the finest bonefishing opportunities in the Bahamas in a spectacular, remote setting. This is a frontier area and it is not uncommon to see schools of bones numbering into the hundreds, many of which have never seen a fly fisherman or fly.

Additional information and booking arrangements for Destinations 7 through 9 may be obtained by contacting, *Angler Adventures,* P.O. Box 872, Old Lyme, CT., 06371, Telephone 203-434-9624 or 1-800-628-1447.

BELIZE

The flats surrounding Turneffe Flats are extensive as well as productive. Fishermen wade and fish from boats during a productive season that goes year-round.

This relatively new country is located just south of Mexico's Yucatan Peninsula, and just east of Guatemala. The Caribbean Sea forms its eastern border. Formerly known as British Honduras, Belize gained its independence from Great Britain in September, 1981. The country is roughly 174 miles long and its greatest width is 68 miles, for a total area of roughly 8,900-square miles, making it the smallest country in Central America. The largest city, also its capital, is Belize City, located on the north-central Caribbean coast, and the point of entry.

Scenically and historically, Belize is rather unique. The coastlands are low and swampy consisting of mangroves and saltwater and freshwater lagoons. The north is low and flat, but in the southeast the elevation rises to 3,000 feet. Some of the best scenery in the country is located in the west, in the Mountain Pine Ridge area. There are also jungle rivers and lush tropical rain forests, home to an array of tropical flowers and wildlife. Nature conservation has become a high priority in Belize, and several nature preserves and national parks have been established. In fact, nature tourism has become the fastest growing industry in the country. Unfortunately, Belize is a poor country. Belize City and other towns resemble typical Third World areas, but beyond that it is an amazing place.

One of the attractions that makes Belize special is its Mayan history. Throughout the country, particularly in the rain forests of the central and southern regions, there are many ruins of the classic Mayan period, which flourished from the 4th to the 9th century. Some of these ruins are being developed as tourist attractions and can be visited and explored. For any angler visiting the country it is well worth the trip. Interested parties should check with their travel agent for details. Of special note is Chiquibul National Park. Covering more than 265,800 acres, it is home to the Mayan ruins of Caracol.

Another phenomenon is the Belize Reef. Stretching more than 180 miles from about the Mexico border south to Sopidilla Cay in the Bay of Honduras, it is the fifth largest barrier reef in the world. In northern Belize around Ambergris Cay, the reef is less than a half mile from shore. This is home to Turneffe Island, Lighthouse Reef and Glover's Reef plus more than 200 other cays, lesser reefs and endless flats. Combined they offer what is acclaimed as some of the world's best permit habitat, and some of the Caribbean's premier angling for bonefish and tarpon.

Traveling to Belize is no more difficult than traveling to Costa Rica, Honduras or the Bahamas. Belize City is serviced by several major carriers from the United States, most connecting through Miami or Houston. All the fishing lodges working in the country make the capital city their point of arrival, and clients are generally met at the airport, assisted through customs and escorted to their hotel or point of departure for the lodge. Basically, Belize is safe, but take the necessary precautions you would anywhere while traveling in Central America or the Caribbean.

TURNEFFE FLATS

Location: Turneffe Island, approximately one hour offshore from Belize City
Capacity: Limited to 14 guests per week
Travel Itinerary: Arrive Belize City, generally on Saturday, and escorted to hotel. Overnight in Belize City and depart for lodge Sunday aboard 31-foot Ocean Master
Accommodations: 6 double occupancy cabins, private bath/hot showers, bar, central dining area, generated 110V/220V AC electrical power, ceiling fans small gift/tackle shop

Primary Fish: Bonefish, permit, tarpon
Size: Bonefish average 2 to 5 pounds, but larger examples up to about 10 pounds are quite possible. Permit run 10 to 15 pounds but fish from 20 to 35 pounds are not unusual. Tarpon average 60 to 90 pounds, but fish in the 100 to 130 pound range are a possibility
Distance to Flats: Within minutes of the lodge or 20 to 30 minutes
Flats-Type: Hard white sand, some soft sand, lots of coral flats and grass. Turneffe has a little bit of everything, but offers some wonderful wading and poling
Boats/Motors: 16 foot Dolphin flats-style skiffs equipped with poling platforms/50hp outboards
Fishing Available: Wading and from boats, depending upon the area, tide, species and other factors. Generally 2 fishermen/1 guide per boat
Areas Fished: Turneffe Island is a maze of over 120 small islands and cays. Extensive flats bless this unique area and nearly all are fished. Some of the best fishing is found along the outside reef and on those flats just inside the reef. Schoolie bones are plentiful on inside flats and are apt to be found anywhere
Notes: Turneffe Flats Lodge is a world-class fishing lodge and the premier resort in the Turneffe area. The guides are all experienced in fly fishing, they know the water extremely well and are experts at locating and spotting fish. It should be noted, Turneffe has been a popular destination for years and has been fished hard. Although there are impressive numbers of bonefish available year-round, they can be wary and difficult at times, but this is not unusual when it comes to bonefish. Permit are also available year-round, and Turneffe has long been considered one of the Caribbean's best spots for this wary fish. Tarpon are considered to be year-round residents as well, but the larger migratory fish begin to arrive in late June, increase in number in July and peak in August. Turneffe is a prime spot to achieve a "Grand Slam" with June through September being the best months. These are the summer months. Fewer anglers visit the area at that time, and fish are less spooky. The migratory tarpon have also arrived and have mixed with the resident tarpon increasing total numbers, and numbers of bones and permit on the flats is also high.

BELIZE RIVER LODGE

Location: Western shore of Belize River, ten minutes from Belize International Airport
Capacity: 16 fishermen/guests
Travel Itinerary: Arrive Belize International Airport, escorted to Belize River Lodge via ground transportation
Accommodations: Four spacious outbuildings constructed of native mahogany, each with ceiling fans, private bath room/showers. Dining room/bar. The grounds are beautifully landscaped, the buildings are surrounded by tropical greenery and exotic flowers
Primary Fish: Bonefish, tarpon, permit
Size: Bonefish run 2 to 4 pounds but larger examples are quite possible. Available year-round. Tarpon average 60 to 80 pounds but larger fish are a good possibility, especially in

August, September and October. The best river fishing for tarpon is February through June, and November and December, with the peak season being April, May and into early June. The best ocean/flats fishing for tarpon is August through October. Permit are available year-round, but August is a particularly good time. Permit average 10 to 25 pounds but examples of 35 and 40 pounds are possible

Distance to Flats: The best bonefish and permit flats are approximately 45 minutes by boat from the lodge. Tarpon can be caught closer to the lodge

Flats-Type: Hard white sand, some soft sand and coral. Turtle grass is also found on some flats

Boats/Motors: 16-18-foot fiberglass skiffs, 2 fishermen/1 guide per boat

Fishing Available: Wading and from boats, depending upon area and angler preference

Areas Fished: Belize River, Sibun River, Black Creek, Manatee River, St. George's Cay and Hickes Cay as well as numerous creeks and lagoons.

Additional information and booking arrangements for Turneffe Flats Lodge can be obtained by contacting: **Turneffe Flats,** P.O. Box 36, Deadwood, S.D., 57732, Telephone 800-815-1304 or 605-578-1304; or, **John Eustice Associates,** 1445 SW 84th Ave, Portland, OR. 97225, Telephone 800-288-0886 or 1-503-297-2468. For infomation on Belize River Lodge contact, **John Eustice Associates** at the above address, or **Angler Adventures,** P.O. Box 872, Old Lyme, CT., 06371, Telephone: 800-628-1447 or 1-203-434-9624.

COSTA RICA

Heading upriver on the Rio Colorado is a journey into a tropical wonderland. Tarpon and other species are found far upstream.

I fell head-over-heels in love with Costa Rica the first time I saw it, and I have been under its magic spell ever since. Located just north of Panama and south of Nicaragua this peaceful, fun-loving country covers about 20,000-square miles, about the same as West Virginia. Despite its small size, howev-

er, there is a great deal to see and do here. There are dense tropical jungles, some of the largest and most unspoiled remaining in Central America, volcanoes, rushing rivers, rugged mountain ranges and sweeping green savannas, all home to more than 12,000 varieties of plants, 237 species of mammals, nearly 850 kinds of birds and more than 360 different amphibians and reptiles. All this, plus borders formed by the Pacific Ocean and the Carribean, create a rich history and a unique philosophy towards country, and preservation of its unique resources.

It was Columbus who first discovered this area in 1502, and gave it its present name which means "Rich Coast." Columbus found no precious gold or silver, but the name was ideally suited for the wealth of natural beauty and climate. The Spaniards colonized the area in the years that followed, and almost all Costa Ricans, who call themselves "Ticos" are of European descent, mostly Spanish. They are a warm, self-assured people, characterized by genuine friendliness making Costa Rica one of the safest countries for visiting and traveling in Central America. Most citizens live in or around San Jose, the capital, located near the heart of the country. Of the two coasts, the Pacific coast is the most developed, with much of the Caribbean shore, except for the port town of Limon, where Columbus is said to have first landed, scattered with small villages or untouched. Costa Rica is also a democracy, the second oldest in the Americas, and it has no army.

But it is more than its people that make this small country such a joy to visit and explore. Two things come to mind. For one, the climate is nearly perfect. Located just ten degrees north of the Equator the average temperature is about 72-degrees F. in the highlands to the low 90s in the lowland. The rainy or "winter" season extends from about May to November, with the dry or "summer" season running from about December through April. There are few biting insects, although do take some insect repellent in case.

And second is Costa Rica's reserved lands, its national parks and wilderness areas. The Talamanca Range traverses the southern part of the country, and includes some of the highest peaks in Costa Rica. Much of the area is preserved in national parks and reserves. In fact, Costa Rica's national park, wilderness and reserve system is the most extensive in Central America, and proportionately, the largest of any country in the Americas. There are more than 25 systems altogether, covering nearly 15 percent of the national territory.

When it comes to angling opportunities, Costa Rica has its share of game fish. On the Caribbean coast, tarpon are "King" among fly fishermen, and though bonefish and permit are not present, the number of year-round tarpon and their size more than makes up. Nor does the tarpon fishing offer the classic sight and cast opportunities so famous in the Florida Keys, Belize and elsewhere. Much of the activity centers around the Rio Colorado, located in the northeast corner of the country, a muddy, silt-loaded drainage where visibility is poor and tarpon are found at deep levels. In most cases, success is just a

matter of getting your fly out, down to the proper level with a full sinking line, and waiting for a hookup. Even in the open salt at the river's mouth, no great casting skills are required.

The reason for visiting the Rio Colorado, however, is that it's one place where tarpon are almost a guarantee, and big tarpon at that. I have personally hooked and landed tarpon over the 100-pound mark, and while the average runs slightly less, this is a great place to learn handling techniques and to feel the power of these great fish. I know of no other place quite like it, and if someone with limited casting skills was to ask where they should go to experience tarpon on a fly rod, one of the lodges on the Rio Colorado would be the place.

RIO COLORADO LODGE

Location: Near mouth of Rio Colorado, northeast corner of Costa Rica
Capacity: 32 fishermen/guests
Travel Itinerary: Arrive San Jose, escorted to hotel for overnight stay; escorted to regional airport for 45-minute charter flight to Barra Colorado. Short walk or boat ride to lodge.
Accommodations: Large spacious bedrooms with single or queen-sized beds, private bath/shower, ceiling fans. Electricity. Large, second floor dining room overlooking the river; bar and game room, including pool table, satellite television, roofed lounge area, tackle shop, zoological gardens throughout the lodge with parrots, macaws and toucans. The entire lodge is under one roof, including access to boats and walkways connecting rooms to dining area and bar.
Primary Fish: Tarpon, (Jack crevalle and snook are also numerous and taken on flies)
Size: Tarpon average 60 to 70 pounds and are available year-round. Much larger examples are common, 150-pound tarpon have been landed
Distance to Flats: No typical flats exist. All fishing is in the river, lagoons or open ocean at the mouth of the river. Traveling time by boat varies from ten to 30 minutes
Flats-Type: See above
Boats/Motors: 23-foot modified V-hull boats with center consoles/285hp Mariner outboards

Fishing Available: Tarpon, from boats, 2 angler/1 guide per boat
Areas Fished: Rio Colorado upstream from lodge, countless lagoons and the open salt at mouth of river
Notes: Rio Colorado Lodge is the oldest and largest tarpon lodge in the area, started by Archie Fields, who gave me my first taste of the area and tarpon fishing in the Rio Colorado. Archie is no longer with us, but I remember his smiling face and warm character fondly. The lodge is the closest to the mouth of the river, where much of the fishing is done, thus offers the shortest running time to that productive area.

Additional information and booking arrangements for **Rio Colorado Lodge** may be obtained by calling toll free, 800-243-9777 in the United States or 813-931-4849 outside the U.S.

SILVER KING LODGE

Location: Rio Colorado, northeast Costa Rica
Capacity: 20 fishermen/guests
Travel Itinerary: same as for Rio Colorado Lodge, except from Barra Colorado a ten minute boat ride to lodge
Accommodations: 20x20 bedrooms with queen-size beds, private bathrooms/showers, ceiling fans. Electricity. Large main dining area, bar, tackle shop, social area.
Primary Fish: See "Rio Colorado Lodge"
Size: See "Rio Colorado Lodge"
Distance to Flats: See "Rio Colorado Lodge"
Type of Flats: See "Rio Colorado Lodge"
Boats/Motors: 19-foot skiffs/40hp Yamaha outboards and 23-foot modified V-hull boats with center consoles/75 hp out boards
Fishing Available: See "Rio Colorado Lodge"
Areas Fished: See "Rio Colorado Lodge"
Notes: Silver King Lodge is the newest tarpon lodge on the Rio Colorado, started in 1991. It is situated just upstream from Rio Colorado Lodge and is a lovely spot with good guides.

Additional information and booking arrangements for **Silver King Tarpon Lodge** may be obtained by contacting: Adventure Marketing, 6107 E-7 Memorial Hwy., Pepper Mound Prof. Center, Tampa, FL., 33615, Telephone 800-450-9908 or 813-249-9908

CUBA

Historic towns and buildings are plentiful.

Despite the fact that it lies just 90 miles south of Florida, for citizens of the United States, Cuba remains the greatest enigma in the Caribbean. On July 8, 1986, just months after the Cuban missile crisis, the U.S. Government issued the Cuban Assets Control Regulations under the Trading With the Enemy Act. In essence, an embargo was set in place, and bans Americans from doing business in Cuba, including traveling there for pleasure.

The embargo is still in effect today, but the walls which once kept this forbidden isle off limits are not as formidable. Although still officially prohibited from doing so, Americans are traveling there, along with a growing number of Canadians, Japanese and Europeans, all of whom have discovered Cuba's many charms. What they find is somewhat surprising, particularly for those visitors just a few miles to the north. In overall appearance, Cuba is a poor country, in many ways Third World. But behind its failing infrastructure is a historically-rich Caribbean isle, one of great beauty and populated by warm and friendly people.

As a tourist attraction, Cuba has light-years to go before it can equal what other Caribbean destinations have to offer. They are working on it, however, and steps have been taken to upgrade accommodations and attractions on some parts of the island,

mostly by foreign concerns. New hotels and resorts have been built, and over the past decade or so the number of visitors has increased substantially each year. When the doors are finally opened to Americans, and this appears more and more likely, Cuba will be of major interest to many.

This is particularly true when it comes to the pursuit of game fish. Hemingway lived and wrote of his angling exploits there, and during Papa Hemingway's day, and for years prior to the embargo, the Isle de Pinos, located off Cuba's western Caribbean coast, was a known hotspot, offering some of the greatest opportunities for bonefish in the Caribbean and to a lesser extent for tarpon. It is said those great schools of bonefish are now gone, fished out by locales. But Cuba has other places where bonefish and tarpon can be considered readily available. I know, for I have seen and fished one of them.

Jardines de la Reina, or Garden of the Queens, is a marvelously enchanting maze of mangrove cays and small isles located about 50 miles off the small seaport of Jucaro, on Cuba's south coast. From the main island, you board a "mother ship," which serves as your home away from home for the duration of the stay. There are no lodges or fancy resorts. No roads, no cars. No neon lights, no telephones or televisions. In fact, the entire archipelago of more than two-hundred cays and tiny islands, which stretch some 120 miles in an east-west direction, is uninhabited. The only air conditioning is the soft tropical winds, and the only entertainment at the end of the day is a sky full of stars so bright it seems you can reach out and grab them, a fine Cuban cigar, a chilled rum and Coke, and the music of water gently slapping against sand and wood. It is a magical place. And despite the rather basic accommodations, "the Garden" is a destination the serious bonefish hunter must experience, for if nothing else it is one of those few places remaining in the Caribbean that time has literally overlooked.

There are schools of bonefish here numbering into the thousands. The average size is two to four pounds, but during my visit I did manage to hook and release several fish of eight and nine pounds, and larger examples were seen. Unlike their counterparts in other Caribbean locales, these fish are also somewhat forgiving. While they will not tolerate major errors in approach or casting, they are uncharacteristically forgiving, and will overlook the many mistakes commonly made by the novice. For that reason, plus the number of bonefish available, "the Gardens" are a great classroom, to say nothing of the simple, unspoiled beauty of the place.

And if bonefish are not enough, tarpon are also available. The largest caught go just under 60 pounds, but the average is much smaller, between 10 and 20 pounds. Despite that fact, fly fishing for them is much like working for tarpon in the backcountry of Florida, beneath overhanging mangroves and around oyster flats, which means they are fun, but always a challenge even for the most advanced caster. There are also lots of them.

JARDINES DE LA REINA (GARDEN OF THE QUEENS)

Location: 50 miles south of Jucaro, Cuba

Capacity: 6 to 8 fishermen

Travel Itinerary: Arrive Jucaro, Cuba, ground transportation to

docking area, and mother ship to Garden of the Queens

Accommodations: 65-foot mother ship offers three double occupancy sleeping quarters, 2 showers and open-deck dining area

Primary Fish: Bonefish and tarpon

Size: Bonefish average 2 to 4 pounds, 10 pound fish possible. Tarpon average 10 to 20 pounds, but examples up to 60 pounds have been taken

Distance to Flats: Just a few minutes from the mother ship, or up to 30 minutes

Flats-Type: Packed sand, some soft sand, coral and lots of turtle grass in some areas

Boats/Motors: 16-foot fiberglass skiffs/40hp Yamaha outboards, one fisherman and one guide per boat

Fishing Available: Wading and from boats

Notes: The Garden of the Queens offers a unique opportunity to see an untouched piece of the Caribbean. The accommodations are basic, but the fishing is some of the best I have ever witnessed. Unless Spanish is spoken, there is a language barrier with the guides, but they are friendly, fun loving locales, who know where to find fish. Fishermen residing in the U.S. should be advised of restrictions pertaining to traveling to Cuba. Interested fishermen may contact: Canada-Cuba Sports and Cultural Festivals, 7171 Torbram Rd, Unit 50, Mississauga, Ont.,Canada L4T 3W4, Tel: 905-678-0426.

FLORIDA

The Florida Keys is blessed with some of the finest guides and equipment in the world. They come at a premium, and are often booked well in advance, particularly during peak season.

There is little doubt that south Florida offers some of the finest fly fishing for bonefish, tarpon and permit on the planet. It is here that many "wannabe" flats fishermen get their start, and where many spend much of their time before venturing to other locales. They learn timing is critical for the best action, as is a good guide for those unfamiliar with the area, but when push comes to shove most agree that for the chance at big fish and clas-

sic sight fishing, particularly for tarpon, this is the place to head for. Most agree, however, there are many other attributes which make this region a top destination.

For one thing, it is easy to reach. Anglers can hop on a plane from virtually any airport in the world and either directly, or through connections, land in Miami on the banks of Biscayne Bay, home to some of the best angling opportunities around. Upon arrival it is also possible to rent a car and head further south to the Keys, that nearly 150-mile-long archipelago of small islands and keys which stretches from Sands, Elliot and Old Rhodes Keys at the south end of Biscayne, all the way to Key West on the Oversea Highway. For those who prefer to fly, smaller airports are also located at Marathon and Key West, with connections in Miami.

Another benefit is the vast array of prime fishing water. There are somewhere between 400 and 500 small islands and keys, many uninhabited and covered with mangrove and pine. Only about 25 are connected and easily reached, but combined they provide some 4,000 square miles of shoal area. Few other places in the world, with the exception of the Bahamas, offer as much territory where bonefish, tarpon and permit can be found. Despite the popularity of the area, the increase in development, and higher numbers of fishermen, there are still places where solitude can be found. This is particularly true on the Gulf side, referred to as the "backcountry," and in the Everglades where tarpon are found in good number.

Lodging, guides and other services are also widely available. There are probably more bonefish, permit and tarpon guides per square mile in the Florida Keys than any other spot on Earth, and an equal number, if not more, of resorts, lodges, hotels, cottages and other places to rest your weary head after a day on the flats. Such places seem to dot U.S. Route 1 from Key Largo to Key West, like pearls on a string, and range from the simple to the sublime. The major centers of activity include Islamorada, Marathon and Key West, and information on accommodations can be obtained by contacting the Chamber of Commerce offices in those towns.

As for guides, they are perhaps the best trained and most knowledgeable anywhere. All must be licensed by the U.S. Coast Guard, and the word "Captain" in front of their name means each one has been tested and deserves that title. I have learned much from these guys over the years, experienced some wondrous things, caught my share of fish, and a number I consider friends.

It must be said, however, while a good many Florida guides go out of their way to educate their clients and show a memorable, as well as productive, fun-filled experience, some seem to take what they do too seriously, and are too intense. Along with that, it is almost as if some guides expect clients to be expert casters and to know and understand the other intricacies required to catch fish in their neck of the woods. When we don't, which is often the case, they don't hesitate to let you know in their own special, sometimes bordering on abusive, if not insulting, way. Fishing the flats is supposed to be fun, and an opportunity to learn something from the best. We are not out there to impress anyone, and hiring a guide

does not mean it's open season on those who know less, or who might not cast like the "pros." It is just fishing, and unfortunately some Florida guides seem to forget that.

For that reason, the best way to hire is through a referral from a friend or acquaintance, someone who has fished with a particular guide before. (Someone like Captain Tony Traad. 28440 SW 192nd Ave., Homestead, FL., 33030, 305-246-0051.) Tony is a trailer guide, which means basically he trailers his 18-foot Hewes Bonefisher to different areas around Flamingo, Biscayne Bay, the Everglades and upper Keys down to Islamorda, depending on where his client is, where the client wants to fish and where the fish are. Another guide worth mentioning is Captain Leon Howell, (31200 S.W. 193rd Ave., Homestead, FL., 33030, Telephone: 305-248-8957). Leon is another trailer guide operating primarily in the Flamingo, Key Biscayne and Everglades area. Further down in Marathon, Captain Dan Strub (305-743-3682), is another friendly, knowledgeable guide. Dan does not specialize in fly fishing, but he is one of the finest tarpon guides I know.

Guides can also be booked through most lodges, resorts and through most tackle and bait shops. In Key West there is *The Saltwater Angler*, 800-223-1629. And in Islamorada the *World Wide Sportsman,* 305-664-4615, and *Florida Keys Outfitters,* 305-664-5423, both make arrangements with area guides. Many guides also advertise in the various fly fishing, and saltwater fly fishing magazines such as *Western Flyfishing, American Angler, Fly Fisherman, Fly, Rod and Reel, Fly Fishing in Saltwaters* and *Saltwater Fly Fishing.* Keep in mind Florida guides are in demand, particularly during peak seasons, so book early.

Compared to opportunities available in other areas in the Caribbean, Florida has a great deal going for it, yet it is not necessarily the best of all worlds. On the plus side are quality guides and accommodations, and the fact that it is close to North Americans and easy to reach by anglers from around the world. There are also good numbers of fish during prime times, and without a doubt few other places provide better sight fishing for tarpon, or offer tarpon potentially as big. The bonefish and permit are also among the largest to be found anywhere.

On the down side, the fishing is not what it once was. The schools of bonefish are not as large as they used to be, and for the novice enthusiast success rates are not as high as they might be in Belize, parts of the Bahamas or Venezuela. Where it is not unusual to hook and play a dozen or more fish in the Caribbean each trip out, in the Keys two or three fish a day is extremely good. Keys bonefish are generally larger, but there are big bones in other areas, too, and comparatively, while bonefish in general are wary, spooky and can be tenacious when it comes to taking a fly, those in the Keys take success to a higher level. They are among the most difficult to dupe with feather and steel and seldom come easy.

The permit fishing is still good, especially around the Marquesas and Key West and around some of the keys just to the north, and big tarpon still come and go with the seasons. Unfortunately, the season is relatively short and while the action can be good, even excellent from April through June or early July,

booking a guide and a place to stay during that period can be next to impossible unless done months in advance.

Fishing the Keys can also be pricey. Guides typically charge $300 to $350 a day for the boat. This cost is generally split between two fishermen, and may come down a little for more than two or three days of fishing, but when you add on lodging, which can vary from a low of $80 per night to $200 per night or more, plus meals and other expenses, the price of a visit quickly rises. At some lodges in the Bahamas, Belize and Costa Rica on the other hand, the cost for a trip may run from $1,500 to slightly over $2,000, but that is for five or six full days of fishing, and meals, lodging, boats and guides are all included.

But with everything considered the Keys are still at the top of the list when it comes to the most popular bonefish, tarpon and permit area in the world. It is where many of us started, and where many newcomers cut their teeth. The important thing is to do your homework, don't set your expectations too high and just go down and have fun.

HONDURAS

Carmen, a guide on the island of Guanaja in Honduras, and the author's wife Diane, work a flat.

Of all the countries in Central America, Honduras is one of the most unique. This is due in part to its lofty mountains, several of which reach an elevation of close to 9,000 feet above sea level. This is the most mountainous and rugged country in Central America. I recall waiting for my flight connection to the island of Guanaja at La Ceiba Airport on the Caribbean Coast, and gazing out at the distant blue volcanic, rainforest-covered mountains and exclaiming how inspiring and beautiful they were. In total area, Honduras covers some 43,277-square miles, and its mountainous central highlands cover more than 65 percent of its national territory. Honduras is bordered on the north by 400 miles of Caribbean shoreline, to the southeast of Nicaragua, on the south by a short stretch of the Pacific and El Salvador, and to the west by Guatemala.

But this country is also unique because of its ancient history. For centuries before the Spanish conquest around 1540, parts of

western Honduras, along with neighboring Guatemala, were home to the Mayan civilization. Excavation digs are ongoing at the Mayan site of Copan, in the far west, on the border of Guatemala, this is a major tourist destination. The site offers interesting observations of religious temples, living quarters and workplaces dating back several hundred years before the arrival of Columbus. In fact, by the time Columbus discovered the mainland of Honduras on his fourth and final voyage to the Caribbean in August of 1502, the Mayans had deserted Copan, Quirigua and other Honduran sites and moved north to the Yucatan where the conquistadors discovered them a short time latter. For anglers traveling to this country, Copan is well worth a side trip. Ask your travel agent for details.

Along its Caribbean coast, Honduras lays claim to several "Bay Islands." The three largest islands include Utila, Roatan and Guanaja. It was the latter where Columbus first landed on July 30, 1502, before touching the mainland two weeks latter. Guanaja is the second-largest of the group, an island covered with pine and tropical forests. There are several beautiful waterfalls, and much of Guanaja Town, the largest settlement, located on a small cay just off the east side of the island, is built on stilts, and bears the nickname, "the Venice of Honduras."

From an angling perspective, Guanaja also provides the best fly fishing opportunities for bonefish and permit. Productive flats are located on both sides of the island, but the most extensive are on the east side, and around several smaller cays within a few-minutes boat ride of the main island. The primary resort is Posada del Sol, or Inn of the Sun, a splendid Spanish-style villa right on the beach facing the Caribbean on the east side. It sits in a magnificent spot, surrounded by rugged hills covered with a dense tropical forest, wild orchids and flowers. It is one of the most beautiful spots I have ever seen in the Caribbean.

Posada del Sol (Inn of the Sun)

Location: Island of Guanaja, Honduras
Travel Itinerary: Arrive Pedro Sula, air connections via Islena Air to La Ceiba or either directly to Guanaja. Visitors are met at the Pedro Sula Airport by a Posada del Sol representative and escorted through customs to necessary connections

Capacity/Accommodations: 24 Spanish-style rooms with tile floors, private bath/shower, terraces Spanish-style dining room, bar, boutique, dive shop, freshwater swimming pool, maid/laundry service, tennis courts
Primary Fish: Bonefish and permit
Size: Bonefish average 2 to 4 pounds, but fish up to 9 pounds have been taken. Double-digit bonefish are possible. Permit average 10 to 20 pounds, larger examples have been taken
Distance to Flats: 10 minutes to one hour, depending upon where you fish. The flats on the west side of the island take the longest to reach. Most flats are within minutes of the resort
Flats-Type: Hard white sand, lots of hard coral and some areas with grass, some soft sand
Boats/Motors: 16-foot fiberglass flat-type skiffs with center consoles/50hp outboards
Fishing Available: Nearly all fishing is by wading
Areas Fished: Several flats along the main island, and around the smaller islands and cays on the east side of the main island. Some isolated flats on the west are also fished
Notes: The island of Guanaja and Posada del Sol make a fine family get-a-way. Hikes to waterfalls and ancient archaeological digs, plus various tours can be arranged. Some of the finest diving in the Caribbean is also available. Generally I would say the fishing for bonefish is fair to good. Large schools of bonefish exist, but chumming by baitfishermen around the smaller outer islands makes success for fly fishermen difficult. Chumming is not done along the main island, however, and these are the areas fly fishermen should concentrate on. My best day has been eight bonefish, the largest about eight pounds. The permit fishing can be excellent, and permit are generally seen each day.

Additional information and booking arrangement for **Posada del Sol** may be obtained by contacting: John Eustice Associates, 1445 SW 8th Ave., Portland, OR. 97225, Telephone: 800-288-0886 or 503-297-2468, or Posada del Sol, 1201 U.S. Highway One, Suite 210, North Palm Beach, FL., 33408, Telephone 800-642-3483 or 407-624-3483

VENEZUELA

Sitting atop the South American continent and facing both the Caribbean Sea and Atlantic Ocean, Venezuela is a paradise-in-waiting for the bonefish and tarpon enthusiast. Much of this vast stretch of shoreline, which covers more than 1,500 miles on the Caribbean and about 300 miles on the Atlantic, is virtually unexplored when it comes to fly fishing opportunities. What has been discovered is generally considered to be some of the most prolific bonefisheries in the world. Tarpon are also present. Two destination of major importance to the fly fisherman include the spectacular area around the bonefish-rich maze of islands of Los Roques, just off the Caribbean coast about 80 miles north of Caracas, the capital. The other tarpon hotspot is Rio Chico, about a three hour drive from the capital, on the mainland.

Largest of the islands in the Los Roques area is El Gran Roque, the point of arrival, home to Macabi Lodge, a small fishing village and not much else. There are no fancy hotels or resorts, no bar, no automobiles and no telephones. Just a pristine island in the middle of nowhere, surrounded by a dozen or so smaller islands and perhaps 100 or more mangrove-covered cays.

Surrounding these islands and cays, however, are dozens of under-fished flats teeming with bonefish. Compared to some flats in Belize and parts of the Bahamas, the typical flat of Los Roques is not huge. Most are perhaps 30 to 50 yards wide and stretch for 100 to 200 yards, but many are larger, and although still narrow may extend for perhaps a mile. Some are coral, some are soft marl covered with turtle grass, but most are hard white sand and combined they provide a wader's paradise. The entire area is part of a national park, development has been curtailed, and fortunately Los Roques will remain the way it is today, forever.

Besides the wading opportunities, what makes this place special is the bonefish themselves. It is not uncommon to see hundreds, if not thousands, of fish each day, the average running about four pounds. Fish over five pounds are caught more frequently than those in the two-pounds-class, and bonefish from seven to 10 pounds are not uncommon. The lodge record is a fish slightly over 13 pounds!

Fishing at Los Roques is particularly good from March through September, generally considered the "prime" months, with May through August perhaps the most consistent period. During the months of December through February, perhaps into early March, good numbers of fish are still available, but cold ocean currents can cool the flats making for inconsistent action. It should be noted, wind is also a factor at Los Roques, and for that reason it may not be the best destination for the novice. Even experienced bonefish hunters should be able to handle a breeze and make accurate casts. Bonefish at Los Roques can be less difficult than their counterparts in other more heavily-fished parts of the Caribbean, but the casting can be more difficult.

Permit are also available, with many running 35 to 45 pounds, although few are caught due in part to the number of bonefish which keep visitors more than occupied. The deeper coral flats to the northeast of the main island are a principal hotspot. Tarpon are present as well, particularly in the deeper channels and on the deeper flats, but again, they are not a hot target. Baby tarpon occupy many of the mangrove lagoons.

The other destination worth mentioning is the tarpon fishery at Rio Chico, technically Tacariqua Lagoon, part of Tacarigua National Park. Basically, this is an area where about a dozen rivers converge and form a massive lagoon system. The entire area is home to thousands of juvenile tarpon, most ranging between two and 20 pounds. Available year-round, larger tarpon in the 20 to 60 pound range are most common from September through November. The water at Rio Chico is somewhat shallow and provides some of the most outstanding surface opportunities for tarpon with poppers and other surface flies to be found anywhere. That, plus the fact that it is not uncommon to land 25 to 50 fish a day, makes this an enjoyable and fun-filled destination.

MACABI LODGE

Location: El Gran Roque Island, Venezuela

Capacity/Accommodations: 12 fishermen and two non-fishermen per week. 10-room villa, with seven double occupancy, air conditioned guest rooms, each with private bath and two twin beds. Main dining area, lounge/bar area

Travel Itinerary: Arrive in Caracas, and overnight, generally at the Melia Caribe, a five-star beachfront hotel only minutes from the airport. Connecting flight the next day to El Grande Roque, about 45-minutes, on twin-engine charter. Clients are met at the airport, helped through customs escorted to the hotel, and to the airport the next day. Same overnight is often required on return

Primary Fish: Bonefish. Permit and tarpon also available but are not heavily sought

Size: Bonefish average 3 to 4 pounds, 7 and 8 pound examples not uncommon with bonefish over 10 pounds possible

Distance to Flats: 20 to 40 minutes

Flats-Type: Coral, soft sand and marl and turtle grass but many are hard white or gold-colored sand

Boats/Motors: 30 foot fiberglass deep-Vee hulls, with twin out boards and radios.

Fishing Available: Nearly all fishing is by wading. One guide per two fishermen

Areas Fished: Flats around El Gran Roque and dozens of other nameless smaller islands and mangrove cays within the proximity

VILLA del MAR

Location: Rio Chico, Tacariqua Lagoon, Venezuela

Capacity/Accommodations: Spacious "efficiency"-style room with range and refrigerator, ceiling fans, bath/shower, open air dining room.

Travel Itinerary: See overnight requirements under "Macabi Lodge"

Primary Fish: Tarpon

Size: Average 2 to 10 pounds. Examples up to 20 pounds common. Larger tarpon in the 25 to 70 pound range seen daily and possible

Distance to Flats: 15 to 30 minutes

Flats-Type: N/A

Boats/Motors: Skiffs/25hp Yamaha outboards, 2 anglers/1 guide per boat

Fishing Available: All fishing is from boats

Areas Fished: The maze of mangrove-lined channels, lagoons and islands of Tacarigua Lagoon, some 10 miles wide and 20 miles long.

Additional information and booking arrangements for **Macabi Lodge** and **Villa del Mar** may be obtained by contacting: Angler Adventures, P.O. Box 872, Old Lyme, CT., 06371, Telephone: 800-628-1447 or 203-434-9624.

YUCATAN PENINSULA, MEXICO

Sticking out into the Gulf of Mexico like a giant horn with the Caribbean forming its eastern border, Mexico's Yucatan Peninsula is a relatively flat piece of real-estate consisting of tangled scub, unrestrained jungle, coral reefs, lagoons and mangrove swamps. Not long ago the place was virtually unknown to much of the angling world, and many areas, particularly the bonefish, permit and tarpon-rich flats in the province of Quintana Roo, along the Caribbean coast, were difficult or impossible to reach. But today, this ancient land of the Maya represents one of the most productive fly fishing destinations in the world.

The area of Ascension Bay is one example. Located about 115 miles south of Cancun, this vast bay and estuary with its miles of unspoiled flats and reefs, is a plane ride and world away from anything else the Yucatan has to offer. A little more than a decade ago, this was a vast wilderness, difficult to reach and with few places to accommodate visiting anglers. That has now changed. An air strip is now found at Punta Pajaros, just minutes away by boat from several first-class fishing lodges, thus making this fragile and unique area available to those hungry seekers of bonefish, permit and tarpon.

When it comes to the "Big Three," Ascension Bay is special. With its extensive flats and rich waters the place undoubtedly provides some of the best bonefish habitat and angling opportunities on the Yucatan. Mudding schools can number into the hundreds, if not thousands. At times they move across the flats in droves and entire flats seem to quiver from their movement. Smaller schools, pairs and large singles are also present, and while the average bonefish in the area runs two to about six pounds, much larger fish are readily available. Bonefish up to 12 pounds have been taken.

Permit and tarpon are also present, in good numbers, and it has been reported Ascension Bay offers the world's largest permit population. Whether this is true or not I cannot honestly say, but like bonefish, permit are available year-round and it is not unusual to spot 20 to 30 permit in a single day, if not more. This is particularly true in the spring and summer months. The average permit runs 10 to 15 pounds, and there are lots of smaller school permit. Much larger fish, some tipping the scales at 30 and 40 pounds, are seen. Permit in this area are quite aggressive compared to those in Florida and other areas, undoubtedly due to the fact that there are so many of them and they are not fished as hard. Though they still demand respect and are not necessarily easy, Ascension Bay is a good destination for the fly fisherman looking for that first permit connection.

Tarpon are here, too and run up to 20 on the average. Tarpon are numerous in the tidal channels, mangrove lagoons and at times on the flats. Larger migratory fish appear in June and remain through the summer. Because bonefish, permit and tarpon are residents of the area, Ascension Bay is a top destination for a "grand slam". The prime time to make the attempt is during late spring and early summer, from late May, and through June and July.

Surrounding Ascension Bay is the one-million-acre Sian Ka'an Biosphere Preserve, established to protect the unique natural surroundings and resources of the area from over development. The Mayans called this place, "birthplace of the sky," and standing on a desolate flat, with not another soul in sight and nothing but the sea touching the sky in all directions, it is easy to understand where the name came from. This is truly a remarkable place, still unspoiled, and one not soon forgotten. It is comforting to know it will remain in its present state for future generations to enjoy and marvel.

CASA BLANCA

Location: Punta Pajaros, on the northern tip of Isla Casa Blanca, at the mouth of Ascension Bay, Yucatan Peninsula, Mexico

Capacity/Accommodations: 18 fishermen/guests. 9 room, most double occupancy with private bath/shower. Some rooms have king-size beds, usually reserved for couples; the other rooms are furnished with double or twin beds, tile floors. Each room has a view of the Caribbean. Bar, main dining room

Travel Itinerary: Arrive Cancun on Saturday, connect with charter plane for 45 minute flight to Punta Pajaros airstrip, then a ten minute boat ride to lodge

Primary Fish: Bonefish, permit, tarpon

Size: Bonefish average 2 to 6 pounds, but examples between 6 and 9 pounds are not uncommon. Bonefish up to 12 pounds have been taken. Permit run 10 to 15 pounds, but large specimens up to 30 and 40 pounds are spotted. The area is blessed with schools of smaller permit. Resident tarpon average under 20 pounds, but in spring and summer migratory tarpon may run 60 to 100 pounds

Distance to Flats: From just in front of the lodge to 45 minutes, depending upon area being fished

Flats-Type: A combination of coral, packed white sands, turtle grass and some soft marl

Boats/Motors: 16-foot fiberglass Dolphin skiffs with forward casting platform and rod storage/30-40hp Yamaha outboards

Fishing Available: Most of the fishing for bonefish and permit is by wading, but some boat fishing is done, depending upon client preference. Tarpon fishing in the mangrove lagoons is generally by boat

Areas Fished: The areas fished are endless. Guides have names for some locales, such as "Tres Marias," "Esperanza" and "Laguna Santa Rosa." Whether named or not, it really makes little difference. Locating secluded, productive places to fish is not difficult

Notes: Casa Blanca is perhaps the premier fishing lodge in the Ascension Bay area. The lodge is top-notch, the guides are knowledgeable, but not all speak fluent English. The lodge is only open from September 29 through July 29. Before or after your visit, a visit to the Mayan ruins at Uxmal, Chicen Itza or Coba might be considered. Ask your travel agent for details.

TIPS FOR FISHING THE FLATS

PREPARING TO CAST

1) Nearly all fishing on the flats is done with a weight-forward floating fly line. Size 6, 7 and 8 are preferred for bonefish; size 7 and 8 are good for permit and small tarpon; and size 10 through size 12 are preferred for large tarpon. Weight-forward-floating lines are easy to cast, load the rod quickly, lift easily off the water and rarely get hung up on the bottom. **Use a neutral or pale color fly line,** gray or sand is best. Very bright lines, especially fluorescent colors, are as easy for the fish to see as they are for you. If you use bright fly lines make sure your leader is long enough to compensate for the line's increased visibilty.

2) When casting from a boat, place a wet towel over any obstructions on the casting deck. Cleats and handles can easily snare your fly line and ruin a good cast or worse, break off a fish or cause bodily injury.

3) Don't strip out any more line than you need to cast or are capable of casting. Make a practice cast, then leave that measured amount of line trailing in the water (if you are wading), or stacked neatly on the deck (if fishing from a boat). This will minimize the amount of line that can tangle on your feet or form knots.

4) Do not stack line on the deck directly from the reel. Instead, make a practice cast, then strip and stack the line. By doing this, the line will shoot front to back, instead of back to front.

5) If casting from a boat, take off your shoes or wear wading socks. This allows you to occasionally feel the line stacked on

Scott Heywood of Sheridan, Wyoming plays a bonefish on a flat near Cooperstown, Abaco, Bahamas.

the deck and you can avoid stepping on it.

6) If using a permanent butt section attached to your fly line with a nail knot, use at least .020 monofilament for size 6 and size 7 lines, size .025 or heavier for size 8 and size .030 for size 10 or larger lines, when using the loop-to-loop connection system. Butt sections of this size will help transfer energy from line to leader much more efficiently.

7) Loop-to-loop connections allow for a quick, easy change of leaders. They are also extremely strong. Attach a two foot section to your fly line, and tie a loop in the end. Depending upon conditions, you can use a pre-looped 7-foot leader if it is windy, or up to a 15-foot leader if it is calm.

8) An 8 or 10-pound test tippet works well for bonefish. For permit 10 to 12-pound test tippets are good and for tarpon shock tippets from 20 to 60-pounds, depending upon size. This is just a general guide, and tippet size can vary depending upon conditions, angler skill and other factors. The important thing is to check for abrasion and test your knots regularly, re-tying your fly after each fish if necessary.

9) Wear footwear when wading, and sunscreen with at least a SPF30.

FLIES

1) The most important aspect of fly selection is sink rate, and secondly is its size. When tying or purchasing flies vary your assortment with flies that are unweighted, flies with bead chain eyes to those with lead barbell eyes, the heaviest. This not only allows you to fish various depths, but also to reach fish that might be tailing in shallow water (light flies), and those fast cruising fish, where casting well ahead of the fish and getting down quickly (heavy flies) might be required. Also vary fly size, since natural foods vary in size and sometimes small flies work when larger sizes don't, and vice versa.

2) Bonefish and permit have an acute sense of smell. Both can smell shrimp and crabs they cannot see. They can also smell insect repellent, sun block, after-shave and gasoline. **Make sure your hands are clean when handling your flies.**

3) **As a general rule, use light-colored flies on light-bottomed flats, dark-colored flies on darker areas,** where turtle grass and coral are dominant. In nature, overt visibility can make any animal prey, and most natural foods are well camouflaged. When it comes to fly size, try smaller flies on fish that are spooky or tailing on clear, shallow flats in calm weather conditions. Sizes 6 and 8 work well for bonefish in these conditions, for example. On deeper flats, or in windy conditions, larger flies work best, as well as on fish that are cruising very fast. Larger flies should always be cast further away from the fish whether it be bonefish, permit or tarpon.

4) **Subtle earth-tone flies (tan, brown, olive, green, gold, yellow) work best on sunny, bright days in shallow water when bonefish are spooky.** Bright flies (pink, orange, chartreuse) work best on cloudy or darker days in deeper water, or latter in the day, especially at sunset.

SEEING AND BEING SEEN

1) **Polarized sunglasses are a must** for spotting fish on the flats. Brown or gray lenses work best on bright days; yellow or amber are best on cloudy, low light days. Side shields will eliminate peripheral light. Make sure you use an eyeglass retainer strap to avoid losing your expensive glasses.

2) **Hats** or a visor to block direct sunlight into the eyes are important, too. The long, bill-type or flats-type hats work well, as do baseball hats.

3) **Always wade quietly and slowly.** This cannot be emphasized enough. Bonefish, permit and even tarpon can "feel" and "hear" water being pushed or splashed by your legs. In most cases, if you can hear water splashing or moving past your legs while wading, you are moving too fast!

4) **Use your eyes; scan constantly.** Anything you think might be a fish, stop and give it careful scrutiny, or even cast to it. You are hunting as much as fishing, pitted against an adversary with an incredible array of sensory organs, and not all fish successfully taken are clearly seen in the beginning.

5) Bonefish and permit especially, have an acute sense of vision. Tarpon have good eyesight as well. Bonefish can see colors well and in a wide variety of light conditions. These fish can also see motion in muddy or clear water, when they are stationary or traveling at top speed. That bright, mango Hawaiian shirt may look great, but under the right conditions fish can see it, too. **Shirts, pants and hats in tan, light blue, light green or other light natural colors will spook fewer fish.** Also remember to remove any bright jewelry.

6) **Use the wind, tide and sun to your advantage.** If possible wade a flat with the wind and sun behind you since it makes casting easier and provides better visibility, and into the current, knowing fish will be working towards you.

7) **Constantly scan the water.** Look for fins, dark, ghost-like shadows, silver flashes below the surface and any surface disturbances such as nervous water, little ripples that look out of place and which work against the surrounding water surface. When trying to spot fish, imagine the water does not exist, looking through it to the bottom, rather than focusing on the surface.

8) **Learn how to cast from your knees or a crouching position.** It may be the greatest asset you have in your arsenal of tricks, particularly when bonefish and permit are close.

WHEN THE EXCITEMENT BEGINS

1) **Always false cast away from the fish,** especially to those slow-moving or tailing fish. This will keep the fly line away from the target area, and reduce your chances of spooking the fish. Cast at a 45 to 90-degree angle in the direction the fish are heading or feeding.

2) **In windy conditions, make your false cast with the rod positioned parallel with, or as close to the water, as possible.** The wind's friction with the water lessens in velocity in the area three to four feet above the surface. This casting technique, which is standard for many flats hunters, makes it harder for the fish to see the fly line and allows for a much quieter presentation of the fly.

3) **Never cast too early.** If possible wait until bonefish and permit are occupied or investigating something to eat. By the same token, never begin your cast when fish are out of range. If the fish moves out of range, be patient. Work to another position and then try again. Never try to cast beyond your range. If you try to cast too long, you might spook the fish, or if it falls short, it simply takes too long to recast.

4) **In nature, prey never moves toward its aggressor. Never place a fly so it is retrieved toward a fish.** Predators chase their prey. They expect their victims to be moving away or stationary, taking up defense. The latter is particularly true with permit hunting crabs.

5) **Learn to strip-strike.** Trout fishermen usually raise the rod tip to strike and set the hook. When used with bonefish, permit and tarpon this technique quickly removes the fly from the fish's field of vision if it has not yet been accepted. A short strip-strike, keeping the rod low and pulling back on the line, might not only give you a second opportunity, but allows the fly to "swim" in a much more lifelike manner.

6) **When retrieving your fly, point the rod tip directly at the fly.** This allows the fly to be imparted with the proper action.

7) **When preparing to make another cast, slowly and quietly lift your line off the water.** Do not use the sudden initiation of the back cast to load the rod tip. Many beginner flats fishermen

do this to help themselves make longer casts, or to cast into the wind. But a quick, splashy lift will spook fish on the flats.

8) Practice casting before heading for the flats. Learn to cast accurately and quickly. False cast as little as possible, keeping in mind the longer the line is in the air the greater the chances of spooking fish. Learn to make two or three false casts, playing out line with each cast and then shooting line accurately.

9) Several clues indicate a fish has taken your fly. Look for rapid fluttering of dorsal fins and tails, fish racing each other to the fly, and most important, if the fish tips down and its tail comes out of the water. With tarpon, you may see a sudden turning, or rolling in the vicinity of your fly. If any of these events take place, count off two or three seconds and strip-strike.

10) If a tarpon or bonefish follows your fly closely but does not take it, a change in your retrieve, either speeding up, slowing down or stopping altogether might induce a second look. With permit, crab flies should be allowed to sit stationary, in a defensive stance, while being investigated. If the fish moves away, however, giving the fly some life, as if it is fleeing the area, will often bring another look.

11) When the fish has been hooked, keep in mind they are fast and powerful. Bonefish can travel almost 30 m.p.h. for several hundred feet in shallow water. Permit aren't nearly as fast, but are much stronger, and hooking into a tarpon is like hooking onto a freight train. Set your drag before you cast, and only with enough tension to put some pressure on the fish and to prevent line from "bird-nesting" in the reel. Too much pressure from the drag too soon will almost assuredly result in breaking the fish off.

12) During the initial power runs, keep your rod low. Allow the fish to run and the drag and lengthening line to increase the pressure. Raise the rod only after the run is over, when retrieving line and actively playing the fish.

13) Once the initial runs are over, it is important to raise the rod and get line back on the reel as quickly as possible. Keep the rod tip high and a steady pressure on the fish, retrieve line only as you pump downward.

14) Keep in mind, the harder you fight a fish, the harder it will fight. Play the fish, but do not overplay the fish. When it wants to run, let it run, retrieving line whenever possible. In the initial stages of the battle maintaining control is next to impossible, but as the fish tires or gets in close, reverse pressure will help terminate the fight. If the fish moves left, work the rod right, and vice versa.

15) Once the battle is over, **handle the fish as little as possible.** Barbless hooks are easily removed, requiring no human contact with the fish. Bonefish will lay near motionless if held belly up, as will permit if held by the tail. For photos, gently handle the fish with wet hands. Bonefish should be handled with one hand firmly around the tail area, the other gently beneath the belly; permit can be handled the same way.

INFORMATION CHART

The following chart has been compiled to offer basic information the traveling angler might find helpful. Only those destinations mentioned in this book are listed, and for anglers traveling to other areas within the Caribbean further research will be required.

While passports are not required by citizens of the United States in all destinations, it is highly recommended that passports always be taken and readily available. I never leave home without it when traveling outside the U.S. For that reason I have indicated passports are required in that category. It should be noted, passport/visa requirements for citizens of Canada and other countries may vary. When booking an angling trip, fishing booking agents and representatives typically inform clients what travel documents are required, but make sure to inquire. Along with passports and/or visas, tourist cards may also be required, and are generally provided by airlines before arrival. Make sure you keep any copies in a safe place and do not lose them, since in some areas they are required for departure. Citizens of the United States should be advised travel restrictions apply for travel to Cuba.

COUNTRY	BELIZE	BAHAMAS	COSTA RICA	CUBA	HONDURAS	MEXICO	VENEZUELA
PASSPORTS	Y	Y	Y	Y	Y	Y	Y
TIME ZONE	CST	EST	CST	EST	CST	CST	EST+1 HR.
OFFICIAL CURRENCY	Belize dollar (BZ$)	Bahamian dollar (B$)	Colon (C$)	Peso (P$)	Lempira (L$)	Peso (N$)	Bolivar (B$)
EXCHANGE RATE	BZ $2=U.S. 1$	par with U.S.	varies in relation to U.S.$	U.S. 1$=0.76 P$	6.17 L$=U.S. 1$ varies	3.12 N$=U.S. 1$	170 B=U.S. 1$
DEPARTURE TAX	11.25$ U.S.	15$ U.S.	7-11$ U.S.	12$ U.S.	Approximately 100L$	12$ U.S.	7-12$ U.S.
OFFICIAL LANGUAGE	English	Spanish/English	Spanish	Spanish	Spanish	Spanish	Spanish
DRY SEASON	February-May	November-April	November-May	November-April	March-August	October-April	November-April
RAIN SEASON	June-July	May-October	June-October	May-October	October-February	May-September	October-April
HURRICANE SEASON	July-November	July-September	—	July-October	—	July-September	—
DUTY FREE CUSTOM ALLOWANCES	200 cigs., or 1/2 lb. tobacco; 20 fl. oz. alcohol	—	200 cigs., 1/4 litre alcohol	200 cigs., or 25 cigars or 1 lb tobacco; 2 bottles alcohol	—	400 cigs., or 1 lb tobacco; 2 bottles alcohol	200 cigs., or 25 cigars; 2 liters alcohol

Exchange rates vary. Check at hotels and banks for best rates. Departure taxes are subject to change most are under $15 U.S. Rain, dry and hurricane seasons may vary. Check with booking agent for details.

FLIES

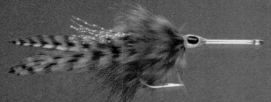

Bob LeMay's Big Eye Tarpon
Orange/Grizzly

Black Death Tarpon Fly

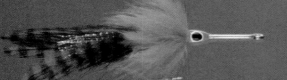

Bob LeMay's Big Eye Tarpon
Orange/Blue

Bob Lemay's Big Eye Tarpon
Furnace/Squirrel

Tim Borski's Orange Butt Tarpon Fly

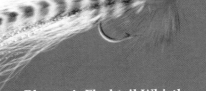

Blanton's Flashtail Whistler

SeaDucer
Red/Yellow

Clouser Deep Minnow
Chartreuse/White

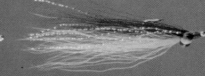

Clouser Deep Minnow
Sculpin

Clouser Deep Minnow
Sculpin

Del Brown's Permit Crab

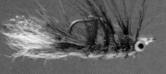

Tim Borski's
Chernobyl Crab

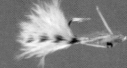

Nix's Epoxy Fly
Pink

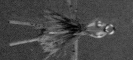

Craig Mathew's
Bonefish Bitter

Crazy Charlie's
Pink

Crazy Charlie's
Tan

Popovics'
Ultra Shrimp

Tim Borski's
Super Swimming Shrimp

IMPROVED CLINCH KNOT

NON-SLIP LOOP KNOT

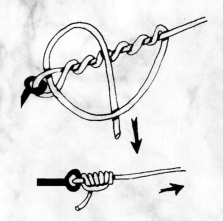

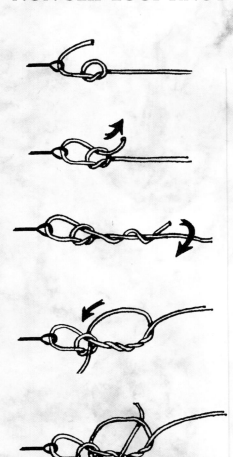

ARBOR KNOT

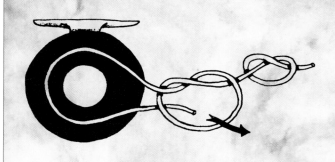

BLOOD KNOT

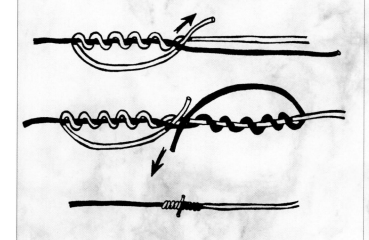

SURGEON"S KNOT

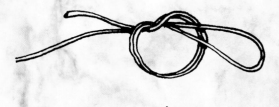

FLY LINE LOOP

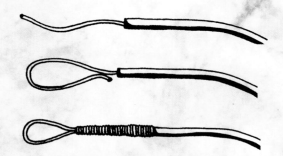

NAIL KNOT

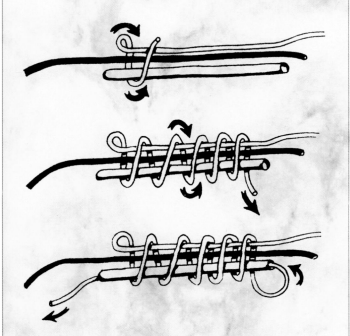

INDEX

BIBLIOGRAPHY

Albury, Paul, *The Story of the Bahamas*, London,
    England, The MacMillian Press, Ltd., 1994
1994 Caribbean Islands Handbook, Bath,
    England, Passport Book
Bates, Joseph, D., Jr., *Fishing, An Encyclopedic Guide*,
    New York, New York, Gramercy Publishing
    Company, 1988
Curcione, Nick, *The Orvis Guide to Saltwater Fly
    Fishing*, New York, New York, Lyons and
    Burford Publishers, 1994
Dalrymple, Byron, *Sportsman's Guide to Game Fish*,
    New York, New York, Outdoor Life
    Books/World Publishing, 1968
Hartwell, George, W., *Fishing Guide to the Bahamas*,
    Miami, Florida, Argos, Inc.
Kaufmann, Randall, *Bonefishing with a Fly*,
    Portland, Oregon, Western Fisherman's Press,
    1992
Kreh, Lefty, *Fly Fishing in Saltwater*, Piscataway,
    New Jersey, Winchester Press, 1986
Kreh, Lefty, *Saltwater Fly Patterns*, New York, New
    York, Lyons and Burford Publishers,
    1995
McClane, A. J., *McClane's Game Fishes of North
    America*, New York, New York, Bonanza
    Books, 1984
McClane, A.J., *McClane's Standard Fishing
    Encyclopedia and International Fishing Guide*,
    New York, New York, Holt, Rinehart and
    Winston, 1965
Meyer, Deke, *Saltwater Flies*, Portland, Oregon,
    Frank Amato Publications, Inc. 1995
Sosin, Mark and Kreh, Lefty, *Fishing the Flats*, New
    York, New York, Nick Lyons Books, 1983
Sosin, Mark and Kreh, Lefty, *Practical Fishing Knots
    II*, New York, New York, Lyons and Burford
    Publishers, 1991
Stewart, Dick and Allen, Farrow, *Flies for Saltwater*,
    North Conway, New Hampshire, Mountain
    Pond Press, 1992
Swisher, Doug and Richards, Carl, *Backcountry Fly
    Fishing in Saltwater*, New York, New York,
    Lyons and Burford Publishers, 1995
Tre Tryckare and Cagner, E., *The Lore of
    Sportsfishing*, New York, New York, Crown
    Publishers, 1976
Wood, Peter, *Caribbean Isles*, New York, New York,
    Time-Life Books, 1975 *Yachtsman's Guide to the
    Bahamas*, North Miami, Florida, Tropic Isle
    Publishers, Inc., 1994

LEARN MORE ABOUT FLY FISHING AND FLY TYING WITH THESE BOOKS

If you are unable to find any of these fine books at your local book store or fly shop you can order direct from the publisher below.

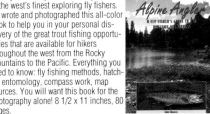